Betty Crocker's
NEW CAKE
DECORATING

Betty Crocker's

NEW CAKE DECORATING

MACMILLAN • USA

Macmillan • USA
A Prentice Hall Macmillan Company
15 Columbus Circle
New York, New York 10023

Library of Congress Cataloging-in-Publication data
Crocker, Betty.
    [New cake decorating]
    Betty Crocker's new cake decorating.
        p.   cm.
    Rev. ed. of: Betty Crocker's cake decorating. ©1990.
    Includes index.
    ISBN 0-671-89748-9
    1. Cake decorating.   I. Title.   II. Title: New cake decorating.
TX771.2.C76   1994
641.8'653—dc20   93-51020
                                                                          CIP

Designed by Levavi & Levavi

Manufactured in the United States of America

10   9   8   7   6   5   4   3   2

First Revised Edition

Front cover: Gingerbread Cake Cottage (page 58), Kitty Cat Cake (page 24), Happy Birthday Cake (page 98)

Back cover: Ballet Slippers Cake (page 14), Train Cake (48)

Contents

Introduction

In our fast-paced world, we often think that we don't have the time to create personalized items or add our special brand of whimsy and fun to everyday life. But, with *Betty Crocker's New Cake Decorating,* you'll find that it's possible—and even fun—to make personalized cakes ranging from the formal to the frivolous.

You'll find wonderful new ways to be creative, and most recipes give instructions for both scratch and mix cakes and frostings, so you can decide how best to spend your time.

We think you'll be delighted with the variety of cakes here. For birthdays, there are traditional cut-out designs, such as the Bunny Cake and the Sailboat Cake, but you'll also be amazed at the range of ideas for cakes, whether for birthdays, office parties, family gatherings or other special events. Try the Electric Guitar Cake for a teenager, the Play Ball Cake for a party to celebrate the World Series and the Fish Cake for your favorite angler.

There is an entire chapter on holiday cakes, with beautiful cakes for Christmas, Halloween, Hanukkah and other holidays, including an easy-to-assemble Gingerbread Cake Cottage. Next are "celebration" cakes for specific events, such as weddings, showers and Father's Day. The cakes are highly versatile—use the Computer Cake to celebrate getting the office on line.

Finally, the section on specialty bakery cakes lets you create stunning cakes that are welcome anytime, such as Lemon Meringue Cake and Decadent Chocolate Cake with Raspberry Sauce.

Every cake is photographed, so you'll know exactly how to make it, plus easy-to-follow line drawings make cutting and assembling any cake a stress-free process.

We think once you find out how easy cake decorating can be, you'll be hooked and enjoy making cakes that personalize events, from a friend's birthday to the Spaceship Cake for someone's who's "out of this world." Whether you like traditional, whimsical or stunning cakes, you'll find them all right here.

THE BETTY CROCKER EDITORS

1

Cut-out
and Shaped
Cakes

Bunny Cake (page 10)

Bunny Cake

It's easy to make "grass" to sprinkle around the bunny. Just shake flaked coconut with a few drops of green food color in a plastic bag.

Carrot Cake (page 146)

Creamy White Frosting (page 151)

Tray or cardboard, 20 × 16 inches, covered

Colored sugar

2 white marshmallow-covered chocolate cake balls with creamy filling

Black shoestring licorice

2 large black gumdrops

1 pink licorice candy

1 large red gumdrop

2 pieces candy-coated gum

2 sticks striped fruit-flavored gum

Bake Carrot Cake was directed for two 8- or 9-inch rounds. Cut one round as shown in diagram. Freeze pieces uncovered about 1 hour for easier frosting if desired. Prepare Creamy White Frosting. Arrange pieces on tray as shown. Frost head and ears with white frosting, attaching pieces with small amount of frosting. Frost tie; sprinkle with colored sugar and outline with shoestring licorice.

Arrange cake balls on frosting for cheeks. Insert short strips of shoestring licorice into cheeks for whiskers. Outline eyes with shoestring licorice; add short strips for eyelashes. Use black gumdrops for pupils of eyes, pink licorice candy for nose, red gumdrop for mouth and gum for teeth. Cut stripped gum into narrow pieces and place in center of ears. Decorate with magician hat and magic wand if desired.

TIME-SAVER TIP: Substitute 1 package (18.25 ounces) yellow cake mix with pudding for the Carrot Cake. Prepare and bake as directed on package. Substitute 2 tubs (16 ounces each) vanilla ready-to-spread frosting for the Creamy White Frosting.

CUTTING AND ASSEMBLING BUNNY CAKE

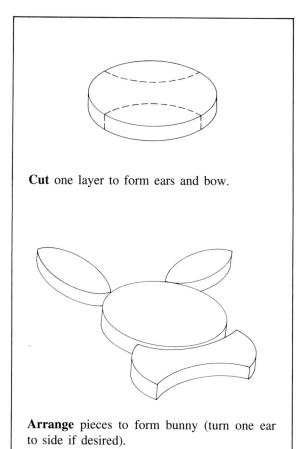

Cut one layer to form ears and bow.

Arrange pieces to form bunny (turn one ear to side if desired).

Athletic Shoe Cake

This cake is in top form for your favorite athlete. You can customize the shoe by using a cup of tinted frosting for the accent color instead of the chocolate frosting. And decorator gel or shoestring licorice can be used to outline the design. If you'd like, use chewy fruit snack cut into ¼-inch-wide strips in place of the licorice for the shoelaces.

Whole Wheat Applesauce Cake (page 145)

Creamy White Frosting (page 151)

Tray or cardboard, 14 × 8 inches, covered

Red paste food color

1 roll grape chewy fruit snack

1 tube (.68 ounce) red decorating gel, if desired

10 ring-shaped hard candies

Red shoestring licorice

Bake Whole Wheat Applesauce Cake as directed for 13 × 9-inch rectangle. Cut cake as shown in diagram. Prepare Creamy White Frosting. Place cake piece 1 on tray; frost top with ½ cup frosting. Place piece 2 on top. Trim one end of shoe to form toe as shown in diagram. Attach pieces 3 and 4 on other end of shoe with small amount of frosting to form high-top opening, trimming to fit and tucking ends of piece 3 inside piece 4. Trim piece 5 and place in high-top opening for tongue. Freeze uncovered about 1 hour for easier frosting if desired. Frost, shaping frosting around piece 5 to resemble tongue. Let frosting set a few minutes. Carefully cover with a paper towel and gently pat to give frosting a fabric-like appearance; remove towel.

Wrap base of shoe with fruit snack. Outline desired markings on shoe with toothpick. Tint remaining frosting desired shade of red; fill in markings. Place ⅓ cup red frosting in decorating bag with writing tip. Trim shoe as desired or trim with decorating gel. Use ring-shaped candies for eyelets and licorice for shoelace. Poke holes in toe and along sides for ventilation holes if desired.

TIME-SAVER TIP: Substitute 1 package (18.25 ounces) yellow cake mix with pudding for the Whole Wheat Applesauce Cake. Prepare and bake as directed on package. Substitute 2 tubs (16 ounces each) vanilla ready-to-spread frosting for the Creamy White Frosting.

CUTTING AND ASSEMBLING ATHLETIC SHOE CAKE

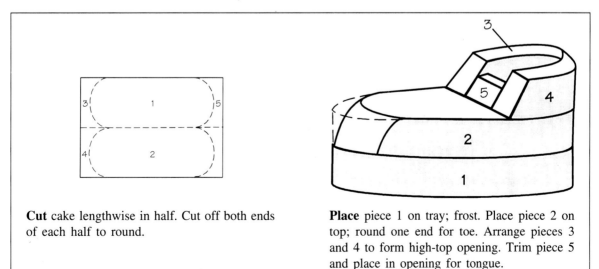

Cut cake lengthwise in half. Cut off both ends of each half to round.

Place piece 1 on tray; frost. Place piece 2 on top; round one end for toe. Arrange pieces 3 and 4 to form high-top opening. Trim piece 5 and place in opening for tongue.

Athletic Shoe Cake (page 11)

Automobile Cake

Automobile Cake

Pound Cake (page 148)

Creamy Vanilla Frosting (page 151)

Desired food color

Tray or cardboard, 13 × 9½ inches, covered

4 cream-filled chocolate sandwich cookies

1 tube (.68 ounce) black or brown decorating gel

Black and yellow licorice beans

1 white and 2 red gum balls

Silver nonpariels

Bake Pound Cake as directed for 2 loaves. Cut and remove 3 inches from end of 1 loaf. Position pieces as shown in diagram for desired automobile. Freeze cut piece uncovered about 1 hour for easier frosting if desired.

Prepare Creamy Vanilla Frosting; reserve ½ cup. Tint remaining frosting with food color. Place whole loaf on tray. Frost top with ⅓ cup colored frosting. Top with cut layer, positioning for desired car. Trim corners for more rounded look if desired. Attach cookies with small amount of frosting for wheels. Draw outline of windows with sharp knife. Frost windows and hubcaps with reserved white frosting. Frost sides and top of car with remaining colored frosting, building up around wheels for fenders.

Outline windows, hood, doors and bumpers with decorating gel. Use licorice beans for grill, door handles and signal lights. Cut gum balls in half; use for headlights and taillights. Make spoke markings on wheel with knife. Press 1 silver nonpariel in center of each wheel. Use silver nonpariels for hood ornament if desired. Remove silver nonpariels before eating.

TIME-SAVER TIP: Substitute 1 package (16 ounces) golden pound cake mix for the Pound Cake. Prepare and bake as directed for 2 loaves. Substitute 1½ tubs (16 ounces each) vanilla ready-to-spread frosting for the Creamy Vanilla Frosting.

CUTTING AND ASSEMBLING AUTOMOBILE CAKE

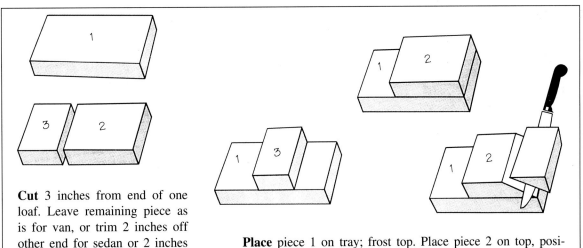

Cut 3 inches from end of one loaf. Leave remaining piece as is for van, or trim 2 inches off other end for sedan or 2 inches diagonally for hatchback.

Place piece 1 on tray; frost top. Place piece 2 on top, positioning for van, sedan or hatchback.

Ballet Slippers Cake

Pipe a special message on the slippers to congratulate an aspiring ballerina on her first recital, her birthday or her graduation from dance school. Decorate with plastic ballet dancers or candies as desired. Meringue powder can be found in most supermarkets today. It is a good substitute for raw egg whites in frostings that need to harden.

Red food color

White Cake (page 149)

Creamy White Frosting (page 151)

Tray or cardboard, 15 × 20 inches, covered

2 yards 1-inch-wide pink ribbon

Bake White Cake as directed for 13 × 9-inch rectangle. Cut cake as shown in diagram. Freeze cut pieces uncovered about 1 hour for easier frosting if desired. Prepare Creamy White Frosting; reserve 1 cup. Tint remaining frosting with 3 drops food color.

Arrange cake pieces on tray. Trim pieces to form slippers. Frost sides of both pieces with pink frosting. Frost top of each piece about 3 inches to the edge for the toes, tapering to about 1 inch around the outside edge for the rest of the slipper. Frost the center oval with reserved white frosting. Let frosting set a few minutes. Carefully cover pink frosting with a paper towel and gently pat to give frosting a fabric-like appearance; remove towel.

Place ½ cup pink frosting in decorating bag with writing tip #5. Pipe a small beaded border where pink frosting edge meets white edge. Pipe a small bow at each toe. Tie ribbon into bow as desired and attach to the back of the slippers.

TIME-SAVER TIP: Substitute 1 package (18.25 ounces) white cake mix with pudding for the White Cake. Prepare and bake as directed on package. Substitute 2 tubs (16 ounces each) vanilla ready-to-spread frosting for the Creamy White Frosting.

CUTTING AND ASSEMBLING BALLET SLIPPERS CAKE

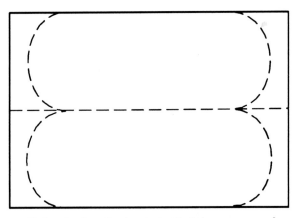

Cut cake lengthwise in half. Trim corners of each half to round.

Ballet Slippers Cake

COLORFUL DESIGNS

Feather Designs: Dip a piece of white sewing thread in liquid food color. Stretch it taut and press lines into frosted cake, using new thread for each color. Immediately draw a knife back and forth across line.

Abstract and Plaid Designs: Dip a piece of white sewing thread in liquid food color. Stretch it taut and press into frosted cake. Repeat, making desired abstract or plaid design. Use new thread for each color.

Tic-Tac-Toe Designs: Dip a piece of white sewing thread in liquid food color. Stretch it taut and press into frosted cake to make tic-tac-toe board. Make x's and o's with candy or cereals.

Bears-on-the-Bus Cake

Yellow Cake (page 150)

Easy Penuche Frosting (page 152)

Tray or cardboard, 15 × 12 inches, covered

1 roll grape chewy fruit snack

30 gummy bear candies

6 ring-shaped hard candies

Chocolate Decorator Frosting (page 150)

2 red cinnamon candies

Bake Yellow Cake as directed for 12 cupcakes and 9-inch square. Cut cake as shown in diagram. Freeze pieces uncovered about 1 hour for easier frosting if desired. Prepare Easy Penuche Frosting. Arrange pieces on tray to form bus as shown in diagram. Frost cake, attaching pieces with small amount of frosting.

Decorate bus with strips of fruit snack as shown in photograph. Press gummy bears in windows.

Press ring-shaped candies on ends of bus for headlights and taillights.

Prepare Chocolate Decorator Frosting. Remove paper baking cups from 2 cupcakes; frost sides and tops with chocolate frosting. Cut narrow slice from each chocolate-frosted cupcake; press cupcakes along bottom of bus for wheels. Press 1 ring-shaped candy with cinnamon candy in center on each wheel.

Frost remaining cupcakes with remaining penuche and chocolate frostings. Press 2 gummy bears on each cupcake. Arrange cupcakes around bus.

TIME-SAVER TIP: Substitute 1 package (18.25 ounces) golden vanilla cake mix with pudding for the Yellow Cake. Prepare as directed on package. Bake as directed in Yellow Cake for 12 cupcakes and 9-inch square. Substitute 1 tub (16 ounces) vanilla ready-to-spread frosting mixed with 7 drops yellow and 1 drop red food color for the Easy Penuche Frosting and ½ tub (16-ounce size) chocolate ready-to-spread frosting for the Chocolate Decorator Frosting.

CUTTING AND ASSEMBLING BEARS-ON-THE-BUS CAKE

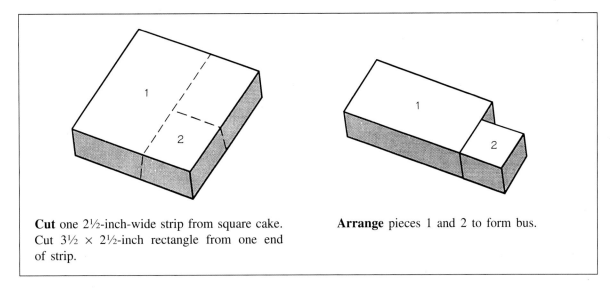

Cut one 2½-inch-wide strip from square cake. Cut 3½ × 2½-inch rectangle from one end of strip.

Arrange pieces 1 and 2 to form bus.

Bears-on-the-Bus Cake

Bicycle Cake

2 recipes Almond Cake (page 149)

Creamy White Frosting (page 151)

Tray or cardboard, 18 × 15 inches, covered

Creamy Chocolate Frosting (page 151)

1 roll strawberry chewy fruit snack

2 fudge-striped cookies with chocolate-covered bottoms

Black liquid paste food color

Prepare 1 recipe Almond Cake as directed for 13 × 9-inch rectangle and 1 recipe as directed for two 8-inch rounds. Cut 13 × 9-inch cake as shown in diagram. Freeze pieces uncovered about 1 hour for easier frosting if desired.

Prepare Creamy White Frosting. Place cake rounds 3 inches apart on tray for wheels. Prepare Creamy Chocolate Frosting. Frost 1-inch-wide strip around edge of each wheel with chocolate frosting; frost centers with white frosting. Arrange

13 × 9-inch piece on tray between wheels. Frost with remaining white frosting. Frost upper left 1½-inch edge with chocolate frosting for seat.

Place 1 cookie in center of back wheel for hub and one between wheels for pedal axle. Tint ¾ cup chocolate frosting with 6 drops food color. Place black frosting in decorator bag with writing tip #3. Pipe spokes and wheel frame on each wheel. Lay strips of fruit snack for bike frame as shown in diagram. Pipe chain and wheel centers with star tip #27. Pipe pedals, handlebars and reflector light holders with writing tip #10. Use small pieces fruit snack for tips of handlebars and reflector lights.

TIME-SAVER TIP: Substitute 2 packages (18.25 ounces each) white cake mix with pudding for the Almond Cakes. Prepare and bake as directed on package. Substitute 1½ tubs (16 ounces each) vanilla ready-to-spread frosting for the Creamy White Frosting and 1 tub (16-ounce size) chocolate ready-to-spread frosting for the Creamy Chocolate Frosting.

Bicycle Cake

CUTTING AND ASSEMBLING BICYCLE CAKE

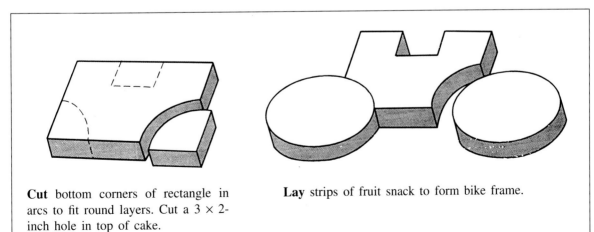

Cut bottom corners of rectangle in arcs to fit round layers. Cut a 3 × 2-inch hole in top of cake.

Lay strips of fruit snack to form bike frame.

Big Burger Cake

For a little extra fun, sprinkle green-tinted, flaked coconut on top of the jelly (to look like shredded lettuce) before putting on the top layer.

> *Pound Cake (page 148)*
> *Peanut Butter Frosting (page 151)*
> *2 tablespoons cocoa*
> *1 to 2 tablespoons strawberry preserves*
> *2 teaspoons toasted sesame seed*

Bake Pound Cake as directed for 1½-quart casserole. Cut cake horizontally into 3 equal layers. Freeze pieces uncovered about 1 hour for easier frosting if desired. Prepare Peanut Butter Frosting. Place bottom layer on serving plate. Frost side only.

Mix ¾ cup of the remaining frosting and the cocoa; if necessary, stir in 1 to 3 teaspoons milk until spreading consistency. Frost top of bottom layer with part of the cocoa frosting. Place middle (hamburger) layer on top; frost top and side of middle layer with remaining cocoa frosting.

Drizzle side of middle layer with preserves to resemble ketchup. Place remaining (rounded) layer on top. Frost with Peanut Butter Frosting. Immediately sprinkle top of cake with sesame seed.

TIME-SAVER TIP: Substitute 1 package (16 ounces) golden pound cake mix for the Pound Cake. Prepare and bake as directed for 1½-quart casserole. Substitute 1 tub (16-ounce size) vanilla ready-to-spread frosting mixed with 7 drops yellow and 1 drop red food color for the Peanut Butter Frosting and ½ tub (16-ounce size) chocolate ready-to-spread frosting for the frosting mixed with cocoa.

FEATHER DESIGNS

Drizzle lines with melted chocolate about 1 inch apart across round frosted or glazed cake. Immediately draw a knife back and forth across lines.

Big Burger Cake

Cheese and Mouse Cake

Carrot Cake (page 146)

Cream Cheese Frosting (page 151)

Yellow and red food colors

Tray or cardboard, 18 × 12 inches, covered

1 pink marshmallow-covered chocolate cake ball with creamy filling

1 large gumdrop

Red shoestring licorice

Strawberry chewy fruit snack

3 miniature chocolate chips

Bake Carrot Cake as directed for 13 × 9-inch rectangle. Cut cake as shown in diagram. Prepare Cream Cheese Frosting; reserve 2 tablespoons. Tint remaining frosting with 2 drops yellow food color. Arrange cake pieces 1 and 2 on tray; frost with ⅓ cup yellow frosting. Place piece 3 on top; frost sides and top.

Put 4 drops yellow food color in custard cup. Dip back of spoon in color; swirl in sides of cake to make holes. Tint reserved frosting pink with 1 drop red food color. Arrange cake ball and gumdrop on top of cake for mouse; frost gumdrop with pink frosting. Use shoestring licorice for tail and whiskers, fruit snack for ears and chocolate chips for eyes and nose.

TIME-SAVER TIP: Substitute 1 package (18.25 ounces) yellow cake mix with pudding for the Carrot Cake. Prepare and bake as directed on package. Substitute 1½ tubs (16 ounces each) cream cheese ready-to-spread frosting for the Cream Cheese Frosting.

CUTTING AND ASSEMBLING CHEESE AND MOUSE CAKE

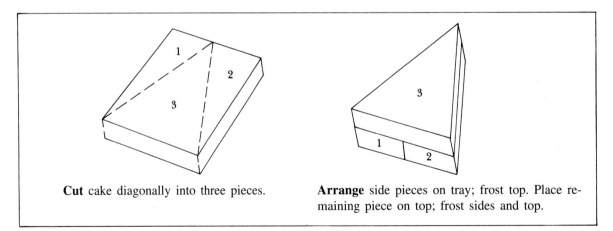

Cut cake diagonally into three pieces.

Arrange side pieces on tray; frost top. Place remaining piece on top; frost sides and top.

Cheese and Mouse Cake and Kitty Cat Cake (page 24)

Kitty Cat Cake

For a tabby cat, lion or Pekinese puppy, tint the coconut the desired color.

> *White Cake (page 149)*
> *Creamy White Frosting (page 151)*
> *Tray or cardboard, 14 × 11 inches, covered*
> *1½ cups flaked or shredded coconut*
> *Red shoestring licorice*
> *Strawberry chewy fruit snack*
> *2 blue jelly beans*
> *1 pink jelly bean*

Bake White Cake as directed for two 8-inch round pans. Cut cakes as shown in diagram. Freeze pieces uncovered about 1 hour for easier frosting if desired. Prepare Creamy White Frosting. Put pieces 1 and 2 together with ⅓ cup frosting. Place cut sides down on tray to form body. Attach remaining pieces with about 1 cup frosting to form kitty as shown in diagram, trimming pieces to fit. Frost cake, shaping cheeks and mouth with small spatula.

Sprinkle with coconut, pressing gently to adhere. Use shoestring licorice for whiskers. Use jelly beans for nose and mouth. Cut ears and tongue from fruit snack. Use remaining fruit snack to make collar and bow. Use licorice beans for eyes.

TIME-SAVER TIP: Substitute 1 package (18.25 ounces) white cake mix with pudding for the White Cake. Prepare and bake as directed on package. Substitute 2 tubs (16 ounces each) vanilla ready-to-spread frosting for the Creamy White Frosting.

CUTTING AND ASSEMBLING KITTY CAT CAKE

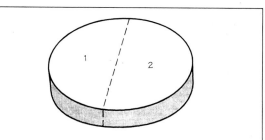

Cut one layer verticaly in half to form body.

Cut second layer to form legs, head, ears and tail.

Arrange pieces from second layer around body to form kitty.

Snowman Cake

Double Chocolate Cake (page 147)

Tray or cardboard, 18 × 10 inches, covered

White Mountain Frosting (page 153)

1 cup flaked or shredded coconut

10 small licorice candies

2 blue licorice candies

1 large black gumdrop, cut in half

1 carrot candy or small piece carrot chewy fruit snack roll-ups

3 chocolate-covered marshmallow cookies

Black shoestring licorice

1 chocolate-covered butter toffee bar

1 pretzel rod

Bake Double Chocolate Cake as directed for one 8-inch round and one 9-inch round. Arrange layers on tray to form snowman. Prepare White Mountain Frosting. Frost, attaching pieces with small amount of frosting.

Sprinkle with coconut, pressing gently to adhere. Use small licorice candies for mouth and buttons, blue licorice candies for eyes, black gumdrop for eyebrows, carrot candy for nose and fruit snack for muffler. Place chocolate-covered cookie on each side of head for earmuffs; attach with shoestring licorice. Cut toffee bar, remaining cookie and pretzel rod in half. Use for legs, shoe and arms.

TIME-SAVER TIP: Substitute 1 package (18.25 ounces) devil's food cake mix with pudding for the Double Chocolate Cake. Prepare and bake as directed on package—except decrease water to 1 cup and stir 1 cup miniature chocolate chips into batter. Substitute 1 package (7.2 ounces) fluffy white frosting mix for the White Mountain Frosting. Prepare as directed on package.

Snowman Cake

Dinosaur Cake

Use multicolored candy-covered chocolate chips or other candies for scales. Colored decorator frosting in a can or tube can be used in place of the decorating gel.

Yellow Cake (page 150)

Creamy Vanilla Frosting (page 151)

Green food color

Tray or cardboard, 18 × 12 inches, covered

1 tube (.68 ounce) black or brown decorating gel

Green candy-coated chocolate chips

Red jelly bean

Bake Yellow Cake as directed for 13 × 9-inch rectangle. Cut cake as shown in diagram. Freeze pieces uncovered about 1 hour for easier frosting if desired. Prepare Creamy Vanilla Frosting; tint with 6 drops food color. Arrange pieces on tray to form dinosaur as shown in diagram. Frost cake, attaching pieces with small amount of frosting.

Let frosting set a few minutes. Carefully cover with a paper towel and gently pat to give frosting a textured appearance; remove towel. Outline scales, legs, mouth, nose and jelly bean eye with decorating gel. Decorate with candy-coated chocolate chips.

TIME-SAVER TIP: Substitute 1 package (18.25 ounces) yellow cake mix with pudding for the Yellow Cake. Prepare and bake as directed on package. Substitute 1½ tubs (16 ounces each) vanilla ready-to-spread frosting for the Creamy Vanilla Frosting.

CANDY BUTTERFLIES

For each butterfly, cut a notch on straight sides of 2 candied fruit slices, slightly below center. Arrange slices for wings and notches for body as shown. Add shoestring licorice for antenna.

Dinosaur Cake

CUTTING AND ASSEMBLING DINOSAUR CAKE

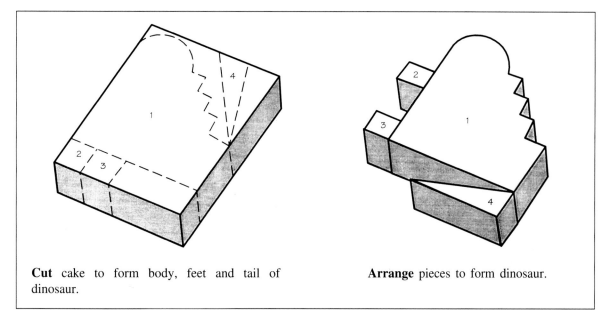

Cut cake to form body, feet and tail of dinosaur.

Arrange pieces to form dinosaur.

Electric Guitar Cake

Cherry-Nut Cake (page 149)

Creamy White Frosting (page 151)

Red paste food color

Tray or cardboard, 20 × 12 inches, covered

Assorted colored sugars

1 red licorice twist

Small silver decorator balls

2 red gumdrops

4 small red round jelly candies

4 capsule-shaped red candies

1 roll strawberry chewy fruit snack

Prepare Cherry-Nut Cake as directed for 13 × 9-inch rectangle. Cut cake as shown in diagram. Freeze cut pieces uncovered about 1 hour for easier frosting if desired. Prepare Creamy White Frosting; reserve ⅓ of frosting. Tint remaining frosting with 10 drops food color. Tint ½ cup red frosting with 2 additional drops food color.

Arrange cake pieces on tray to form guitar. Frost top and side of neck and sounding board with white frosting, reserving ¼ cup frosting.

Frost the rest of the cake with the lighter red frosting. Sprinkle sounding board with colored sugars. Place deeper red frosting in decorating bag with writing tip #4. Pipe frets on neck. Pipe beaded border around sounding board where the red and white frostings meet.

Pipe 2 rows of stars, 3 inches long, for bridge with the ¼ cup reserved white frosting and star tip #18. Cut licorice twists into 3-inch lengths; place on sounding board as shown. Place silver balls on neck between frets as shown. Add gumdrops for control knobs, small candies for string pegs and the capsule-shaped candies at the top side edge for tuning pegs. Cut 4 pieces of fruit snack ⅛ inch wide by 18 inches long with a knife and a straight edge. Place the strings on the cake, tucking ends into the bridge and wrapping other ends around the top and side pegs. Cut strings ¼ inch from each tuning peg, tucking the tails into the frosting.

TIME-SAVER TIP: Substitute 1 package (18.25 ounces) yellow cake mix with pudding for the Cherry-Nut Cake. Prepare and bake as directed on package. Substitute 2 tubs (16 ounces each) vanilla ready-to-spread frosting for the Creamy White Frosting.

Electric Guitar Cake

CUTTING AND ASSEMBLING ELECTRIC GUITAR CAKE

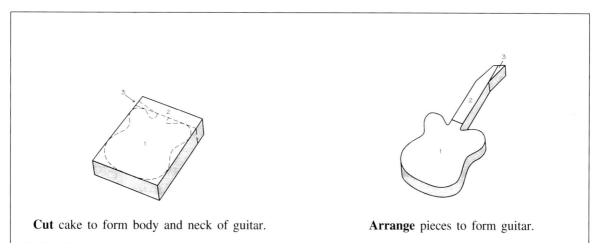

Cut cake to form body and neck of guitar.　　　　**Arrange** pieces to form guitar.

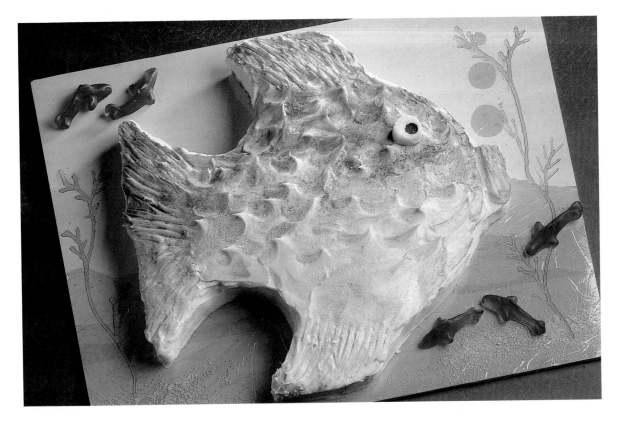

Fish Cake

CUTTING AND ASSEMBLING FISH CAKE

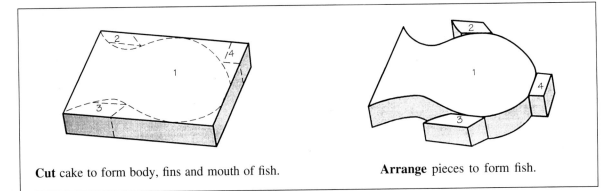

Cut cake to form body, fins and mouth of fish.

Arrange pieces to form fish.

Fish Cake

Anglers and tropical fish lovers will be hooked on this cake! For a fun presentation, cover the board with blue plastic wrap and decorate with green frosting for seaweed. Add sea creatures and shells as desired.

Lemon–Poppy Seed Cake (page 150)

Tray or cardboard, 18 × 13 inches, covered

Creamy Citrus Frosting (page 151)

Blue, green and yellow food colors

Yellow sugar

1 yellow and black round licorice candy

Bake Lemon–Poppy Seed Cake as directed for 13 × 9-inch rectangle. Cut cake as shown in diagram. Freeze pieces uncovered about 1 hour for easier frosting if desired. Arrange pieces on tray to form fish as shown in diagram. Prepare Creamy Citrus Frosting. Frost cake, attaching pieces with small amount of frosting.

Drop 5 drops green food color along center of fish. Drop 4 drops blue food color along top of fish, 4 drops green along center and 4 drops yellow along bottom. Starting from top edge of fish, blend colors into frosting, working blue down into green and green down into yellow. Use back of spoon to form scales. Define lips with edge of spatula. Mark tail and fins with fork. Sprinkle bottom half of fish with yellow sugar. Use licorice candy for eye.

TIME-SAVER TIP: Substitute 1 package (18.25 ounces) yellow cake mix with pudding for the Lemon–Poppy Seed Cake. Prepare and bake as directed on package. Substitute 1 tub (16-ounce size) vanilla ready-to-spread frosting for the Creamy Citrus Frosting.

FLOWER DESIGNS

Drizzle round frosted or glazed cake with melted chocolate, beginning with small circle in center and encircling with larger circle, ½ inch outside the other. Immediately draw a knife from outside edge inward and from center outward alternately 4 to 8 times.

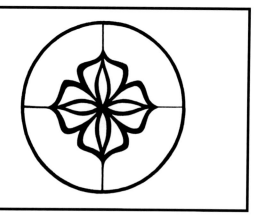

Gum Ball Machine Cake

Dip the tops of the cupcakes in colored sugars, if you like, instead of coloring them with food color. Jumbo gum balls or other round candies can be used if you don't have a small cupcake pan.

> *Almond Cake (page 149)*
>
> *Creamy Almond Frosting (page 151)*
>
> *Blue, green, red and yellow food colors*
>
> *Tray or cardboard, 17 × 12 inches, covered*
>
> *1 tube (.68 ounce) red decorating gel*

Bake Almond Cake as directed for 12 small cupcakes, 8-inch round and 8-inch square. Cut cake as shown in diagram. Freeze pieces uncovered about 1 hour for easier frosting if desired. Prepare Creamy Almond Frosting.

Frost each cupcake with scant tablespoon frosting. Place 1 drop blue food color in center of each of 3 cupcakes. Spread color through frosting. Repeat with green, red and yellow food colors and remaining cupcakes. Arrange cake pieces on tray to form gum ball machine as shown in diagram. Frost piece 1 with ⅔ cup frosting. Place cupcakes on top.

Tint remaining frosting with 7 drops yellow food color. Frost remaining pieces, attaching them with small amount of frosting. Outline workings of machine as desired with red gel.

TIME-SAVER TIP: Substitute 1 package (18.25 ounces) yellow cake mix with pudding for the Almond Cake. Prepare and bake as directed for assorted pans. Substitute 1½ tubs (16 ounces each) vanilla ready-to-spread frosting for the Creamy Almond Frosting.

CUTTING AND ASSEMBLING GUM BALL MACHINE CAKE

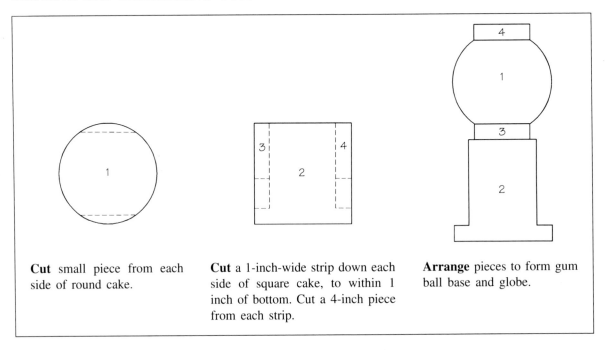

Cut small piece from each side of round cake.

Cut a 1-inch-wide strip down each side of square cake, to within 1 inch of bottom. Cut a 4-inch piece from each strip.

Arrange pieces to form gum ball base and globe.

Horse's Head Cake

Marble Cake (page 149)

Creamy Chocolate Frosting (page 151)

Tray or cardboard, 14 × 10 inches, covered

2 large black gumdrops

⅓ cup powdered sugar

1 teaspoon milk

1 teaspoon margarine or butter, softened

Bake Marble Cake as directed for two 9-inch rounds. Reserve 1 layer for another use. Cut cake as shown in diagram. Freeze pieces uncovered about 1 hour for easier frosting if desired. Prepare Creamy Chocolate Frosting. Arrange cake pieces on tray to form horse's head as shown in diagram; trim pieces 2 and 3 to form ears.

Frost cake, attaching pieces with small amount of frosting. Place gumdrops on face for eyes. Use fork to draw hair into frosting, bringing frosting up over gumdrops to form eyelids. Mark nose indentations with small spatula. Mix powdered sugar, milk and margarine. Brush on face between ears and eyes with fork to form forelock.

TIME-SAVER TIP: Substitute 1 package (18.25 ounces) marble cake mix with pudding for the Marble Cake. Prepare and bake as directed on package. Substitute 1 tub (16-ounce size) chocolate ready-to-spread frosting for the Creamy Chocolate Frosting.

Horse's Head Cake and Monkey Cake (page 36)

CUTTING AND ASSEMBLING HORSE'S HEAD CAKE

Cut cake to form horse's face and ears.

Arrange pieces to form horse's head.

CUTTING AND ASSEMBLING MONKEY CAKE (page 36)

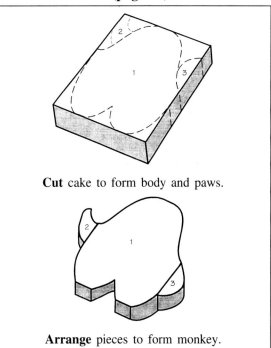

Cut cake to form body and paws.

Arrange pieces to form monkey.

Monkey Cake

Dark Cocoa Cake (page 147)

Creamy Cocoa Frosting (page 151)

½ cup powdered sugar

2 teaspoons milk

Tray or cardboard, 16 × 14 inches, covered

Miniature chocolate chips

2 banana chips

1 pecan half

1 banana-shaped candy

Bake Dark Cocoa Cake as directed for 13 × 9-inch rectangle. Cut cake as shown in diagram. Freeze pieces uncovered about 1 hour for easier frosting if desired. Prepare Creamy Cocoa Frosting. Mix 1 tablespoon frosting, the powdered sugar and milk; reserve.

Arrange pieces on tray to form monkey as shown in diagram; trim pieces 2 and 3 to fit for arms. Draw outline of face with sharp knife. Frost sides and top of cake, except face, with cocoa frosting, attaching pieces with small amount of frosting. Make lines in frosting with tines of fork to resemble fur. Fill in face with reserved frosting, reserving 2 tablespoons. Place reserved frosting in decorating bag with writing tip #4. Pipe outlines of hands and face. Use chocolate chips for eyebrows, banana chips for eyes, pecan half for nose and banana candy for mouth. Place banana-shaped cookie in monkey's hand if desired.

TIME-SAVER TIP: Substitute 1 package (18.25 ounces) devil's food cake mix with pudding for the Dark Cocoa Cake. Prepare and bake as directed on package. Substitute 1½ tubs (16 ounces each) chocolate ready-to-spread frosting for the Creamy Cocoa Frosting.

In-line Skate Cake

If you want to make a cake for an ice-skating party, just eliminate the wheels and brake.

Almond Cake (page 149)

Creamy Almond Frosting (page 151)

Green and yellow food colors

Tray or cardboard, 18 × 15 inches, covered

1 roll strawberry chewy fruit snack

4 fudge-striped cookies with chocolate-covered bottoms

1 tube (.68 ounce) black or brown decorating gel

8 ring-shaped hard candies

Bake Almond Cake as directed for 13 × 9-inch rectangle. Cut cake as shown in diagram. Freeze pieces uncovered about 1 hour for easier frosting if desired. Prepare Creamy Almond Frosting. Tint ⅓ cup frosting with 3 drops green food color. Arrange pieces on tray to form skate as shown in diagram, trimming pieces to fit. Frost cake with white frosting, attaching pieces with small amount of frosting.

Outline inner throat and tongue of skate with toothpick. Tint 2 tablespoons white frosting with 2 drops yellow food color; frost inner throat. Frost tongue and back of throat with green frosting. Use fruit snack to form brake, strap and back of throat. Make 4 slits in bottom edge of blade and insert cookies for wheels. Outline skate and blade with decorating gel (outline first with toothpick if desired). Use ring candies for eyelets and wheel axles. Cut ¼-inch wide strips of fruit snack and use for laces.

TIME-SAVER TIP: Substitute 1 package (18.25 ounces) white cake mix with pudding for the Almond Cake. Prepare and bake as directed on package. Substitute 1½ tubs (16 ounces each) vanilla ready-to-spread frosting for the Creamy Almond Frosting.

In-line Skate Cake

CUTTING AND ASSEMBLING IN-LINE SKATE CAKE

Cut a 2-inch-wide strip from one end of cake; trim end at a diagonal for back end of wheel case. Cut remaining piece of cake to form boot, front end of wheel case and brake stop.

Arrange pieces to form in-line skate.

Panda Cake

Marble Cake (page 149)

Tray or cardboard, 16 × 10 inches, covered

White Mountain Frosting (page 152)

½ cup flaked coconut

8 chocolate wafers, about 2 inches in diameter

1 large marshmallow

2 chocolate-covered candies

1 small black or red gumdrop

Black shoestring licorice

⅓ cup flaked coconut

1 teaspoon cocoa

Bake Marble Cake as directed for one 8-inch round and one 9-inch round. Cut 9-inch round as shown in diagram. Arrange pieces on tray to form panda as shown in diagram.

Prepare White Mountain Frosting. Frost cake, attaching pieces with small amount of frosting. Sprinkle body with ½ cup flaked coconut, pressing gently to adhere. Press 2 wafers into top of head at 45° angle for ears. Place 2 wafers for background of eyes and 4 on body for paws, placing bottom 2 wafers at 45° angle on bottom edge of cake.

Cut marshmallow crosswise in half; place each half on a chocolate wafer for eyes. Place chocolate candies on marshmallow halves for pupils; fasten with small dab of frosting if necessary. Use small gumdrop for nose and shoestring licorice for mouth and outline of legs. Toss ⅓ cup coconut and the cocoa; carefully sprinkle within outline of legs and on bottom portion of body.

TIME-SAVER TIP: Substitute 1 package (18.5 ounces) fudge marble or devil's food cake mix with pudding for the Marble Cake. Prepare and bake as directed on package. Substitute 1 package (7.2 ounces) fluffy white frosting mix for the White Mountain Frosting. Prepare as directed on package.

CUTTING AND ASSEMBLING PANDA CAKE

Cut small piece from one side of 9-inch layer.

Join 8-inch layer to cut section of 9-inch layer.

Panda Cake

Play Ball Cake

This cake will feed the whole team! The Baseball Caps can be eliminated if you just want a ball. For a basketball, tint the frosting orange and use licorice laces for a basketball design. For a soccer ball, outline the design with a toothpick and fill in every other section with desired colored frostings.

2 recipes Yellow Cake (page 150)

Creamy White Frosting (page 151)

Tray or cardboard, 15 inches round, covered

Red shoestring licorice

Baseball Caps (right)

Decorating gel, if desired

Bake 1 recipe Yellow Cake as directed for 1½-quart casserole. Repeat with second recipe. Prepare Creamy White Frosting. Place 1 cake, rounded side up, on tray. Trim top to make a flat surface. Spread with ⅓ cup frosting. Trim top of second layer flat. Place upside down on top of first layer to make a ball. Frost entire cake. Use red licorice for seams on baseball as shown. Pipe desired message with decorating gel.

BASEBALL CAPS

Double Chocolate Cake (page 147)

Creamy White Frosting (page 151)

Assorted food colors

Black shoestring licorice

Candy-coated fruit pieces

Assorted candied fruit slices

Decorating gel, if desired

Bake Double Chocolate Cake as directed for cupcakes. Prepare Creamy White Frosting. Divide frosting among small bowls for as many colors as desired. Stir 2 drops desired food color into frosting in each bowl. Trim top of each cupcake to make a flat surface. Frost bottoms and sides of cupcakes with assorted colored frostings. Place as many cupcakes around baseball as will fit. Place remaining cupcakes on separate tray. Starting at center top of each cap, place pieces of black shoestring licorice down sides for seams. Place 1 candy-coated fruit piece at center top. Use fruit slices for brims (trim fruit slices if necessary). Pipe child's name or team initial on caps if desired.

TIME-SAVER TIP: Substitute 1 package (18.25 ounces) yellow cake mix with pudding for the Yellow Cake and 1 package (18.25 ounces) devil's food cake mix with pudding for the Double Chocolate Cake. Prepare and bake as directed on package. Substitute 5 tubs (16 ounces each) vanilla ready-to-spread frosting for the Creamy White Frosting and Buttercream Frosting.

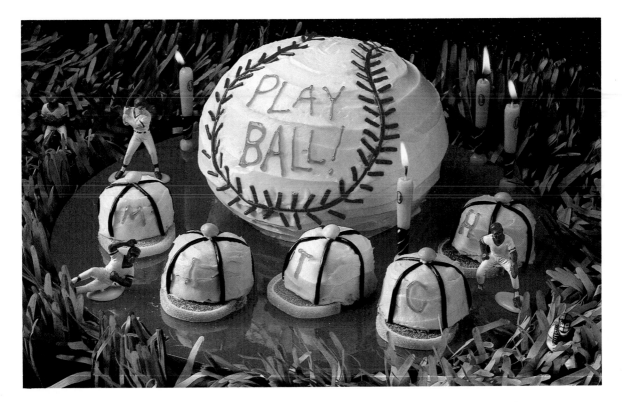

Play Ball Cake

PATCHWORK DESIGNS

Mark servings in the frosting of a square or rectangular cake with a knife or toothpick. Fill the squares with chopped nuts, miniature candy-coated chocolate chips or pieces, confetti candy bits, crushed candies, colored sugars, fruit-shaped candies, tinted coconut, chopped dried fruits, chocolate-dipped fruits, small shaped cookies or crackers or cereals.

Sailboat Cake

Buttermilk Spice Cake (page 146)

White Mountain Frosting (page 153)

Tray or cardboard, 20 × 18 inches, covered

1 tablespoon cocoa

14 × 4-inch piece of aluminum foil*

5 ring-shaped hard candies

Bake Buttermilk Spice Cake as directed for 13 × 9-inch rectangle. Cut cake as shown in diagram. Freeze pieces uncovered about 1 hour for easier frosting if desired. Prepare White Mountain Frosting; reserve 1 cup. Arrange pieces on tray to form sailboat as shown in diagram, leaving space between sails for mast. Frost sails with remaining frosting.

Gently fold cocoa into frosting until blended. Frost hull of sailboat with cocoa frosting. Roll up aluminum foil for mast; place between sails. Use ring-shaped candies for portholes.

TIME-SAVER TIP: Substitute 1 package (18.25 ounces) spice, devil's food or yellow cake mix with pudding for the Buttermilk Spice Cake. Prepare and bake as directed on package. Substitute 1 package (7.2 ounces) fluffy white frosting mix for the White Mountain Frosting. Prepare as directed on package.

*A 14 × 4-inch piece of wrapping or shelf paper can be substituted for aluminum foil; secure with tape.

CUTTING AND ASSEMBLING SAILBOAT CAKE

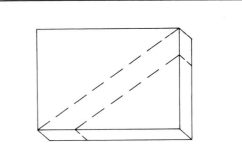

Cut cake diagonally into three pieces.

Arrange pieces to form sailboat, leaving space between sails for mast.

Sailboat Cake

Spaceship Cake

Yellow Cake (page 150)

Creamy Vanilla Frosting (page 151)

Tray or cardboard, 17 × 12 inches, covered

1 roll strawberry chewy fruit snack

1 tube (.68 ounce) black decorating gel

Bake Yellow Cake as directed for 13 × 9-inch rectangle. Cut cake as shown in diagram. Freeze pieces uncovered about 1 hour for easier frosting if desired. Prepare Creamy Vanilla Frosting.

Place cake piece 1 on tray. Frost with about 1¼ cups frosting. Arrange pieces 2, 3 and 4 as shown in diagram, trimming to fit, standing up piece 3 for top fin. Trim point of piece 2 for nose of ship. Frost cake with remaining frosting. Let frosting set a few minutes. Carefully cover with a paper towel and gently pat to give a fabric-like appearance; remove towel. Use fruit snack for strips as shown in photograph. Outline as desired with decorating gel.

TIME-SAVER TIP: Substitute 1 package (18.25 ounces) yellow cake mix with pudding for the Yellow Cake. Prepare and bake as directed on package. Substitute 1½ tubs (16 ounces each) vanilla ready-to-spread frosting for the Creamy Vanilla Frosting.

CUTTING AND ASSEMBLING SPACESHIP CAKE

Cut cake to form body pieces of space ship.

Place piece 1 on tray; frost. Arrange remaining pieces to form space ship, standing up piece 3 for top fin.

Spaceship Cake

Teddy Bear Cake

You can use a lollipop, candy cane or other candy instead of the ice cream cone, or you can eliminate it altogether.

Double Chocolate Cake (page 147)

Creamy Chocolate Frosting (page 151)

Tray or cardboard, 17 × 12 inches, covered

1 roll strawberry chewy fruit snack

2 large black gumdrops

2 large red gumdrops

Red shoestring licorice

Pink nonpareil candies

6 medium red gumdrops, cut in half

½ ice cream cone

Bake Double Chocolate Cake as directed for one 8-inch round and one 9-inch square. Cut cake as shown in diagram. Freeze pieces uncovered about 1 hour for easier frosting if desired. Prepare Creamy Chocolate Frosting. Arrange pieces on tray to form a teddy bear as shown in diagram. Frost cake, attaching pieces with small amount of frosting, reserving 2 tablespoons frosting.

Make fur marks in frosting with fork, leaving face smooth. Cut tongue, ears and bow from fruit snack. Use black gumdrops for eyes, large red gumdrop for nose and licorice for mouth. Accent bow with other large red gumdrop. Sprinkle nonpareils on cheeks and paws. Use 3 medium gumdrop halves for pads on each paw. Position ice cream cone, cut side down, between top paws for honey pot. Place reserved frosting in decorating bag with writing tip #3. Pipe *honey* on cone.

TIME-SAVER TIP: Substitute 1 package (18.25 ounces) devil's food cake mix with pudding for the Double Chocolate Cake. Prepare and bake as directed on package—except decrease water to 1 cup and stir 1 cup miniature chocolate chips into batter. Substitute 1 tub (16-ounce size) chocolate ready-to-spread frosting for the Creamy Chocolate Frosting.

CUTTING AND ASSEMBLING TEDDY BEAR CAKE

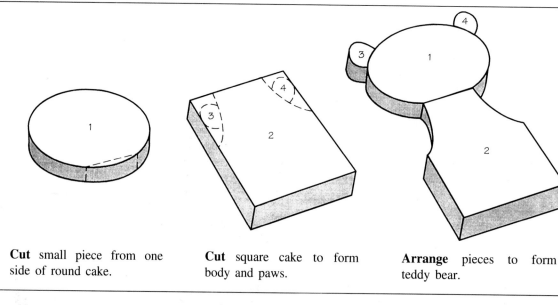

Cut small piece from one side of round cake.

Cut square cake to form body and paws.

Arrange pieces to form teddy bear.

Teddy Bear Cake

Train Cake

Double Chocolate Cake (page 147)
Creamy Chocolate Frosting (page 151)
Tray or cardboard, 25 × 13 inches, covered
4 black-and-white striped licorice candies
8 pink-and-black round licorice candies
Black shoestring licorice
4 cream-filled chocolate cookies
1 round pink licorice candy
2 black cylinder-shaped licorice candies
2 pieces popcorn
1 solid chocolate drop in foil wrapping
3 teddy bear-shaped cookies
5 sticks red licorice twists
Semisweet rainbow morsels
Creamy Vanilla Frosting (page 151)
Fruit-shaped cookies or crackers
6 yellow-and-black round licorice candies
Animal-shaped cookies or crackers
10 candy sticks (3 inches)
Yellow and red food colors
1 round blue licorice candy

Bake Double Chocolate Cake as directed for two 9-inch loaves. Cut cake as shown in diagram, being careful not to cut all the way through piece 1 when removing piece 2. Trim pieces 3 and 6 flat on top. Freeze pieces uncovered about 1 hour for easier frosting if desired. Prepare Creamy Chocolate Frosting.

Arrange cake pieces 1 and 2 on tray to form engine, stacking piece 2 on top for engine house, as shown in diagram. Frost with chocolate frosting. Cut each black-and-white striped licorice candy into thirds. Place on front of engine, slanting outward to simulate a cow catcher. Cut 6 pink-and-black round licorice candies in half; use for wheels. Connect front wheels with small pieces of black shoestring licorice. Attach cream-filled chocolate cookies on engine with small amount of frosting to sim-

ulate a boiler. Place pink licorice candy on front of boiler for headlight. Attach black cylinder-shaped licorice candies to boiler for smokestack. Attach popcorn with frosting to smokestack to simulate smoke. Use unwrapped solid chocolate drop for bell and teddy bear-shaped cookies for engineers. Outline top edge of coal car with licorice twists and fill with semisweet rainbow morsels.

Prepare Creamy Vanilla Frosting. Place piece 3 on tray for log car. Frost car with ½ cup vanilla frosting. Stack with candy sticks to simulate logs. Cut 2 yellow-and-black round licorice candies in half; use for wheels.

Place piece 4 on tray for animal car. Trim top round if desired. Tint ½ cup vanilla frosting with 6 drops yellow food color; frost car. Place animal-shaped cookies on top of car and in window outlined with shoestring licorice. Cut 2 pink-and-black licorice candies in half; use for wheels.

Place piece 6 on tray for fruit car. Frost with ½ cup vanilla frosting. Fill with fruit-shaped candies. Cut 2 yellow-and-black licorice candies in half; use for wheels.

Place piece 5 on tray for caboose. Trim to make shorter and rounded on top if desired. Tint ½ cup vanilla frosting with 2 drops red food color. Frost car, placing a mound of frosting on top of caboose. Cut 2 yellow-and-black licorice candies in half; use for wheels. Use black shoestring licorice to outline railing and door on caboose. Use small piece of black cylinder-shaped licorice candy for windows and door handle. Place blue licorice candy and teddy bear-shaped cookie on top. Connect cars together with pieces of licorice twists.

TIME-SAVER TIP: Substitute 1 package (18.25 ounces) chocolate fudge cake mix with pudding for the Double Chocolate Cake. Prepare and bake as directed for loaf pans. Substitute 1 tub (16-ounce size) chocolate ready-to-spread frosting for the Creamy Chocolate Frosting and 1 tub (16-ounce size) vanilla ready-to-spread frosting for the Creamy Vanilla Frosting.

Train Cake

CUTTING AND ASSEMBLING TRAIN CAKE

Engine side view.

Cut narrow strip lengthwise from each side of one loaf. Remove a 1½-inch-wide, 1½-inch-thick section from piece 1, being careful not to cut all the way through (see side view).

Cut second loaf crosswise into fourths.

Festive Holiday Cakes

Holiday Pinecone Cake (page 52)

Holiday Pinecone Cake

Carrot Cake (page 146) and two recipes of Cream Cheese Frosting (page 151) can also be used to make this stunning holiday cake.

2 cups powdered sugar

2 tablespoons meringue powder

¼ cup water

Green food color

Pumpkin-Gingerbread Cake (page 148)

Creamy White Frosting (page 151)

2 tablespoons cocoa

6 horn-shaped corn snacks

Tray or cardboard, 16 × 12 inches, covered

1 tube (.68 ounce) red decorating gel

Draw a pair of lines, 1½ inches apart, down the length of a page of ruled paper. Make 2 more pairs. Place under sheet of waxed paper. Beat powdered sugar, meringue powder and water with standard mixer on medium speed or with hand mixer on high speed about 7 minutes or until stiff peaks form. Tint with 3 drops green food color. (Stir in ½ teaspoon cocoa if desired for a dull green color.) Place in decorating bag with writing tip #5. Pipe 140 pine needles, 1½ inches long, inside each pair of lines using the rules as a guide. Allow to dry at least 8 hours.

Bake Pumpkin-Gingerbread Cake as directed for 13 × 9-inch rectangle. Prepare Creamy White Frosting. Mix cocoa and 1 cup frosting. Place a corn snack on waxed paper. Starting at pointed end, pipe three petals in a circular motion with cocoa frosting and petal tip #104. Continue making petals, 1 row at a time, alternating and adding loops to shape pinecone. Finish with the bottom row, completely covering open end of corn snack. Repeat with the 5 other corn snacks. Allow to dry several hours.

Place cake on tray. Reserve 1¾ cups frosting. Frost top of cake with remaining white frosting. Pipe a shell border around base of cake with 1 cup reserved white frosting and star tip #5. Pipe a double shell border around top edge of cake with white frosting and star tip #18.

Carefully remove pinecones from waxed paper and arrange on cake in upper left and lower right corners. Pipe pine branches with remaining cocoa frosting with writing tip #5. Tint ½ cup of the remaining white frosting with 3 drops green food color. Pipe holly leaves with green frosting and leaf tip #67. Pipe desired message on cake with red decorating gel. Pipe red dots for holly berries on lettering and on holly leaves. Carefully remove pine needles from waxed paper and insert them around pinecones and along branches.

TIME-SAVER TIP: Substitute 1 package (18.25 ounces) yellow cake mix with pudding for the Pumpkin-Gingerbread Cake. Prepare and bake as directed on package.

Christmas Tree Cake

White Cake (page 149)

White Mountain Frosting (page 152)

Green food color

Tray or cardboard, 15 × 13 inches, covered

1 chocolate-coated butter toffee bar

1 tube (.68 ounce) green decorating gel

1 large yellow gumdrop

Nonpareil mint chips

Bake White Cake as directed for 13 × 9-inch rectangle. Cut cake as shown in diagram. Freeze pieces uncovered about 1 hour for easier frosting if desired. Prepare White Mountain Frosting.

Arrange cake pieces 1 and 2 on tray; frost. Place piece 3 on top; frost sides and top. Dip fork into food color and draw through frosting to create boughs. Insert toffee bar into end of tree to make trunk. Draw light strings with decorating gel. Roll yellow gumdrop on heavily sugared surface into circle ⅛ inch thick; cut into star and place at top of tree. Place nonpareil mint chips on strings for lights.

TIME-SAVER TIP: Substitute 1 package (18.25 ounces) white cake mix with pudding for the White Cake. Prepare and bake as directed on package. Substitute 1 package (7.2 ounces) fluffy white frosting mix for the White Mountain Frosting. Prepare as directed on package.

CUTTING AND ASSEMBLING CHRISTMAS TREE CAKE

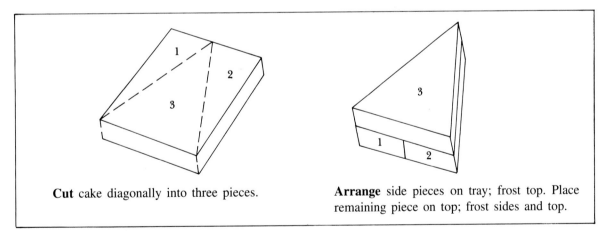

Cut cake diagonally into three pieces.

Arrange side pieces on tray; frost top. Place remaining piece on top; frost sides and top.

Mini Bûche de Noël Cakes 🌿

These mini logs are simple enough for children to make. For a more elegant look, decorate the finished cakes with Chocolate Twigs (page 144) and Chocolate Leaves (page 78) and dust with cocoa. They can also be decorated with gumdrop hatchets for President's Day.

White Cake (page 149)
Creamy Chocolate Frosting (page 151)
About 12 Gumdrop Hollies (right)

Bake White Cake as directed for 24 cupcakes. Prepare Creamy Chocolate Frosting. Put 2 cupcakes together end-to-end with small amount frosting to make logs. Frost sides, leaving ends unfrosted. Make strokes in frosting with fork to resemble bark. Arrange 1 Gumdrop Holly on each log.

TIME-SAVER TIP: Substitute 1 package (18.25 ounces) devil's food cake mix with pudding for the Dark Cocoa Cake. Prepare and bake as directed on package. Substitute 1½ tubs (16 ounces each) chocolate ready-to-spread frosting for the Creamy Chocolate Frosting.

CHRISTMAS DESIGNS

Gumdrop Holly: For each holly, roll 2 or 3 large green gumdrops, one at a time, on heavily sugared surface until ⅛ inch thick. Cut to resemble holly leaves. Arrange leaves close together; add 3 red cinnamon candies for holly berries.

Holiday Jelly Bells: Tint 2 tablespoons orange marmalade with 2 drops green food color, and 1 tablespoon orange marmalade with 3 drops red food color. Mark 3 bells, using bell-shaped cookie cutter, on top of cake frosted with white frosting. Fill 2 bells with green marmalade and 1 bell with red marmalade. Dip toothpick into additional green food color and draw lines to connect bells.

Mini Brûche de Nöel Cakes and Christmas Tree Cake (page 53)

Holiday Quilt Cake

This quilt design is lovely for any occasion: Use pastel colors for showers and bright colors for birthdays.

> *Chocolate-Cherry Cake (page 147)*
>
> *Tray or cardboard, 16 × 12 inches, covered*
>
> *Creamy Vanilla Frosting (page 151)*
>
> *1 tube (4.25 ounces) green decorating icing*
>
> *1 tube (4.25 ounces) red decorating icing*
>
> *Assorted candies and colored sugars*

Bake Chocolate-Cherry Cake as directed for 13 × 9-inch rectangle. Place cake on tray. Prepare Creamy Vanilla Frosting. Frost cake with remaining white frosting, reserving 1 cup.

Pipe lines with green or red icing to divide cake into 24 squares. Decorate every other square with tinted frostings, candies or sugars as desired to resemble quilt pattern. Place reserved frosting in decorating bag with star tip #18. Pipe border around top and bottom edges of cake.

TIME-SAVER TIP: Substitute 1 package (18.25 ounces) devil's food cake mix with pudding for the Chocolate-Cherry Cake. Prepare and bake as directed on package—except fold ½ cup chopped maraschino cherries, well drained, into batter. Substitute 1½ tubs (16 ounces each) sour cream or vanilla ready-to-spread frosting for the Creamy Vanilla Frosting.

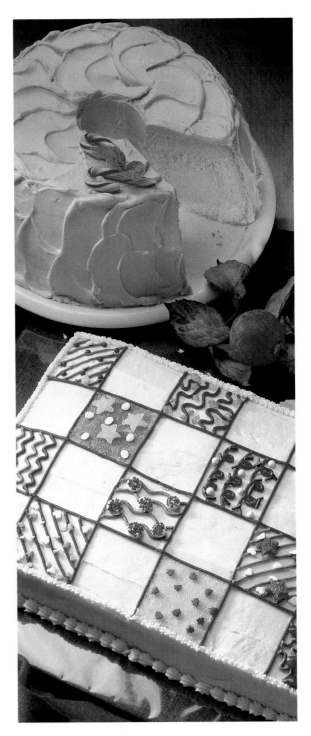

Holiday Quilt Cake and Peppermint Whipped Cream Cake

Peppermint Whipped Cream Cake

Angel Food Cake (page 145)
3 cups whipping (heavy) cream
1½ cup powdered sugar
1 teaspoon peppermint extract
Red food color
3 tablespoons crushed peppermint candy
  or 2 small candy canes

Bake Angel Food Cake as directed. Remove cake from pan; place upside down. Slice off top of cake about 1 inch down and reserve. Cut down into cake 1 inch from outer edge and 1 inch from edge of hole, leaving substantial walls on each side. Remove center with a spoon or curved knife, being careful to leave a base of cake 1 inch thick.

Beat whipping cream, powdered sugar, peppermint extract and 12 drops food color in chilled bowl until stiff. Spoon two-thirds of the whipped cream into cake cavity. Press mixture firmly into cavity.

Replace top of cake and press gently. Frost cake with remaining whipped cream. Refrigerate at least 4 hours. Just before serving, sprinkle with crushed candy or arrange candy canes on top. Garnish with fresh mint if desired. Refrigerate any remaining cake.

TIME-SAVER TIP: Substitute 1 package (16 ounces) white angel food cake mix for the Angel Food Cake. Prepare and bake as directed on package.

CUTTING AND FILLING PEPPERMINT WHIPPED CREAM CAKE

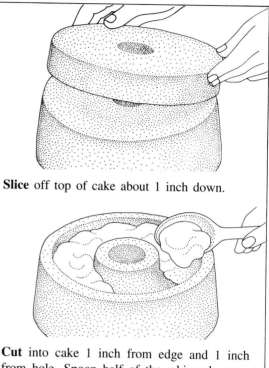

Slice off top of cake about 1 inch down.

Cut into cake 1 inch from edge and 1 inch from hole. Spoon half of the whipped cream into cavity of cake.

Gingerbread Cake Cottage

This adorable cottage can be made out of any flavor 13 × 9-inch rectangle cake. Use it as a housewarming gift, and decorate it to match the new house!

> *Pumpkin-Gingerbread Cake (page 148)*
>
> *2 recipes Easy Penuche Frosting (page 152)*
>
> *Creamy Vanilla Frosting (page 151)*
>
> *Tray or cardboard, 12 × 9 inches, covered*
>
> *3 green striped candy sticks (5 inches each)*
>
> *3 or 4 chocolate sugar wafer cookies (4½-inch length)*
>
> *2 green licorice beans*
>
> *4 vanilla sugar wafer cookies (4½-inch length)*

Prepare and bake Pumpkin-Gingerbread Cake as directed. Prepare frostings. Cut cake as shown in diagram. Assemble cake pieces on tray with about 1½ cups Easy Penuche Frosting to hold pieces together. Place piece 1 on tray; frost top. Frost top of piece 2; top with piece 3. Stand pieces 2 and 3 upright on piece 1. Trim corners and base so pieces fit smoothly. (Roof point will be slightly off center.) Place cake in freezer; freeze until firm.

Remove cake from freezer. Frost exterior of house with remaining 2½ cups Easy Penuche Frosting. Use the end of a small spatula to press lines on front of cottage to simulate logs. Smooth frosting on front, sides and back of house with slightly dampened large spatula.

Place about ⅓ cup Creamy Vanilla Frosting at a time in decorating bag with writing tip #6. Break one striped candy stick in half. Pipe a strip of frosting down the length of each candy stick half. Press one half to each vertical front edge of house. Attach remaining candy sticks along front roof lines. Let set about 30 minutes.

Cut chocolate wafer cookies to make doors and shutters. Attach with small amount of frosting piped to the back of each piece. Pipe outlines of window panes and frames. Attach licorice beans for door handles. Trim shutters with decorative sprinkles if desired.

Cut vanilla sugar wafer cookies to make chimney pieces. The back piece should be 1½ inches in length, the front piece 2½ inches in length. For the sides, cut two pieces each 2 inches in length. Cut one end of each piece at an angle, so that the side facing the back measures 1½ inches in length and the side facing the front measures 2½ inches in length. Pipe frosting on inside vertical edges of two slanted chimney pieces. Press side pieces of chimney into frosting to form box. Hold a few minutes until set; let dry. Pipe frosting on bottom edges of chimney; place on roof.

Pipe any remaining frosting along roof lines, around base of chimney and around front corners of house and doors with writing tip #10 to create snowdrifts. Let set about 30 minutes.

Gingerbread Cake Cottage

CUTTING AND ASSEMBLING GINGERBREAD CAKE COTTAGE

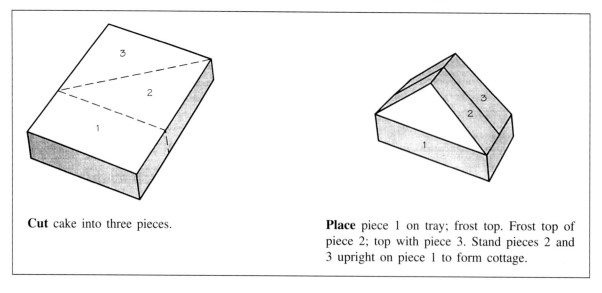

Cut cake into three pieces.

Place piece 1 on tray; frost top. Frost top of piece 2; top with piece 3. Stand pieces 2 and 3 upright on piece 1 to form cottage.

New Year's Eve Confetti Cake

1 roll strawberry chewy fruit snack

1 roll grape chewy fruit snack

5 Party Blowers (page 61)

Cherry-Nut Cake (page 149)

Creamy Vanilla Frosting (page 151)

Assorted sugar sequins

Assorted colored sugars

3 candy sticks (5 inches)

Unroll and cut narrow 12-inch piece from each fruit snack roll. Cut each piece lengthwise into 4 strips with a knife and a straightedge. Roll each strip in a spiral around handle of a wooden spoon. Store at room temperature at least 8 hours to set curl to make streamers. Make Party Blowers.

Bake Cherry-Nut Cake as directed for 2 rounds. Prepare Creamy Vanilla Frosting; reserve ¼ cup for Party Blowers. Fill layers and frost cake. Press colored sugar sequins and sugars into frosting on side and along outer edge of top of cake.

Place Party Blowers on top of cake with candy sticks toward center of cake. Unwrap streamers from spoon handles. Reshape into desired curl and place between Party Blowers and around base of cake.

TIME-SAVER TIP: Substitute 1 package (18.25 ounces) white cake mix with pudding for the Cherry-Nut Cake. Prepare and bake as directed on package. Substitute 1½ tubs (16 ounces each) vanilla ready-to-spread frosting for the Creamy Vanilla Frosting.

Chocolate Heart Cake

Dark Cocoa Cake (page 147)

Fluffy Cocoa Frosting (page 152)

Tray or cardboard, 18 × 15 inches, covered

Gumdrop Rose (page 88)

Chocolate Leaves (page 78)

Bake Dark Cocoa Cake as directed for one 8-inch round and one 8-inch square. Prepare Fluffy Cocoa Frosting. Cut round layer in half. Arrange pieces on tray to form heart as shown in diagram. Frost cake, attaching pieces with small amount of frosting. Decorate with Gumdrop Rose or fresh rose sprinkled with powdered sugar and Chocolate Leaves.

TIME-SAVER TIP: Substitute 1 package (18.25 ounces) devil's food cake mix with pudding for the Dark Cocoa Cake. Prepare and bake as directed on package.

CUTTING AND ASSEMBLING CHOCOLATE HEART CAKE

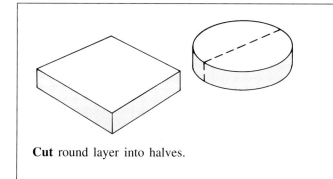

Cut round layer into halves.

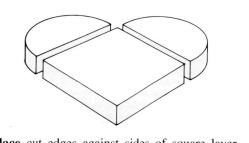

Place cut edges against sides of square layer to form heart.

PARTY BLOWERS

For each blower, break a 5-inch candy stick in half. Cut a 4-inch piece from a roll of chewy fruit snack. Place a small amount of frosting ¼ inch from broken end of 1 candy stick half. Wrap narrow end of piece of fruit roll over frosting. Pipe 2 rows of frosting stars over seam with star tip #30. Curl the end of the fruit roll to about 1½ inches from star rows and secure with small amount of frosting if needed.

New Year's Eve Confetti Cake

Cake Full of Hearts

How about a cake full of pumpkins, dinosaurs, bells, angels or stars? Use any shape cookie cutters and any color candy sprinkles for birthdays, hobbies, showers or holidays.

Cherry-Nut Cake (page 149)

Creamy Vanilla Frosting (page 151)

Red food color

Tray or cardboard, 16 × 12 inches, covered

Heart-shaped cookie cutters

Assorted nonpareils, colored sugars and sprinkles

3 ounces red cinnamon candies

Bake Cherry-Nut Cake as directed for 13 × 9-inch rectangle. Prepare Creamy Vanilla Frosting; reserve ½ cup. Tint remaining frosting with 3 drops food color; reserve ½ cup. Place cake on tray. Frost top and sides of cake.

Place various sizes of heart-shaped cookie cutters on cake. Sprinkle nonpareils, colored sugars and sprinkles inside cutters, pressing gently onto frosting. Carefully remove cookie cutters. Outline largest hearts with cinnamon candies. Place cinnamon candies along base of cake.

Tint reserved pink frosting with 3 additional drops food color. Place frosting in decorating bag with writing tip #4. Pipe beaded border around smaller hearts. Pipe beaded border along outside edge of cake with reserved white frosting. Add a few cinnamon candies or heart-shaped candies between hearts if desired.

TIME-SAVER TIP: Substitute 1 package (18.25 ounces) white cake mix with pudding for the Cherry-Nut Cake. Prepare and bake as directed on package. Substitute 1½ tubs (16 ounces each) vanilla ready-to-spread frosting for the Creamy Vanilla Frosting.

COOKIE CUTTER DESIGNS

Outlined Designs: Press cookie cutters into frosted cake; outline markings with small candies. Or, dip cookie cutters in liquid food color; lightly press cutters into frosted cake.

Filled-in Designs: Place cookie cutters on frosted cake, sprinkle inside cutter with colored sugar, small candy sprinkles or small candies. Gently press into frosting; remove cookie cutters.

Cake Full of Hearts and Chocolate Heart Cake (page 61)

CUTTING AND ASSEMBLING EASTER BUNNY CAKE

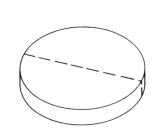

Cut cake into halves to make two semicircles.

Cut notch about one-third of the way up one edge of body to form head.

Attach cut out piece for tail with toothpick.

Cut 4 × 1¾-inch ears from pink construction paper. Fold as shown.

Easter Bunny Cake

Carrot Cake (page 146)
White Mountain Frosting (page 152)
Tray or cardboard, 12 × 8 inches, covered
1 cup shredded coconut
Jelly beans or small gumdrops
1 cup shredded coconut
Green food color
Pink construction paper

Bake Carrot Cake as directed for 8- or 9-inch rounds. Reserve 1 layer for another use. Prepare White Mountain Frosting. Cut 1 layer in half as shown in diagram. Put halves together with frosting to form body. Place cake upright on cut edge of tray.

Cut a notch about one-third of the way up one edge of body to form head as shown in diagram. Attach cut-out piece for tail with toothpicks. Frost with remaining frosting, rounding body on sides. Sprinkle with 1 cup coconut. Cut ears from construction paper; press into top. Use jelly beans for eyes and nose.

Shake 1 cup shredded coconut and 3 drops food color in tightly covered jar until evenly tinted. Surround bunny with tinted coconut. Add additional jelly beans if desired.

TIME-SAVER TIP: Substitute any 8- or 9-inch cake layer for the Carrot Cake. Substitute 1 package (7.2 ounces) fluffy white frosting mix for the White Mountain Frosting. Prepare as directed on package.

Easter Bunny Cake

Easter Cross Cake

5 ounces almond paste

Red, green and yellow food colors

Purple paste food color

2 cups powdered sugar

2 tablespoons meringue powder

¼ cup water

Almond Cake (page 149)

Creamy White Frosting (page 151)

Tray or cardboard, 20 × 15 inches, covered

To make lilies, knead and roll out half of the almond paste ⅛ inch thick. Trace lily pattern; cut out 3 lilies. Holding lily in palm, gently roll into a cone shape, overlapping seam. Curl petals out and down. Dilute few drops red food color with water. Brush red strips from the base up the center of each lily petal with a small brush. Roll a 1-inch ball of paste into a 2½-inch bud. Knead 2 drops green food color into remaining almond paste. Roll out to ⅛ inch thickness. Cut out 5 leaves about 3 inches long. Place on sheet of waxed paper, shaping to curl slightly. Allow lilies and leaves to dry at least 8 hours.

Beat powdered sugar, meringue powder and water with standard mixer on medium speed or with hand mixer on high speed about 7 minutes or until stiff peaks form. Tint ½ cup meringue icing with 3 drops yellow food color; reserve. Tint remaining icing with paste food color. Place purple icing in decorating bag with petal tip #190. Pipe 15 purple flowers onto waxed paper. Pipe 9 small purple flowers with petal tip #223. Pipe 18 stamens, about 1¾ inches long, with yellow icing and writing tip #4. Allow flowers and stamens to dry at least 8 hours. Store the decorating bag and tip with the yellow icing in an airtight container for cake assembly the next day.

Bake Almond Cake as directed for 13 × 9-inch rectangle. Cut cake as shown. Freeze cut pieces uncovered about 1 hour for easier frosting if desired. Prepare Creamy White Frosting. Tint ½ cup frosting with 2 drops red food color. Tint ½ cup frosting with 2 drops green food color.

Arrange cake pieces on tray to form cross as shown in diagram. Reserve ½ cup of the white frosting. Frost top and sides with remaining white frosting. Spread a 1-inch-wide strip of pink frosting, ¼ inch thick, up one side of

CUTTING AND ASSEMBLING EASTER CROSS CAKE

Cut cake lengthwise in half. Cut a 4-inch-long piece from the end of one half for piece 3.

Arrange pieces to form cross.

Trace lily pattern.

Easter Cross Cake

decorating bag. Fill bag with reserved white frosting. Pipe shell border with star tip #32 along top edge and base of cake, holding bag so pink strip is toward the outside.

Pipe a small amount of yellow meringue icing inside each lily at the base; insert 5 stamens in icing in each lily. Place lilies and bud on cake. Place green frosting in decorating bag with writing tip #5. Pipe stems to each lily; pipe long stem along left side of cake. Arrange leaves along stem. Arrange large and small purple flowers on top of cake. Pipe small flowers to fill in with remaining pink frosting and star tip #18. Pipe leaves around some of the flowers with green frosting and leaf tip #67. Pipe a small dot of yellow icing in center of each flower.

TIME-SAVER TIP: Substitute 1 package (18.25 ounces) white cake mix with pudding for the Almond Cake. Prepare and bake as directed on package.

Pot-o'-Gold Cake

Paste food color gives the bright, sharp colors needed for the rainbow. Liquid food color will have a softer look.

Applesauce Cake (page 145)

Creamy White Frosting (page 151)

Red, yellow, blue and green paste food colors

2 tablespoons cocoa

Tray or cardboard, 18 × 14 inches, covered

⅓ cup shredded coconut

Green liquid food color

8 butterscotch hard candies, crushed

60 small round green candies

Bake Applesauce Cake as directed for 13 × 9-inch rectangle. Cut cake as shown in diagram. Freeze cut pieces uncovered about 1 hour for easier frosting if desired. Prepare Creamy White Frosting. Tint 2 cups frosting red with paste color and 1 cup frosting each yellow, blue and green with paste colors. Mix cocoa and remaining 1 cup frosting.

Arrange cake pieces on tray to form rainbow, pot and grass as shown in diagram. Frost top edge and side of the rainbow with red frosting. Frost the center with yellow frosting. Frost bottom edge and side with blue frosting. Frost top of the pot yellow. Draw a fork through frosting, following curve of rainbow.

Reserve ¼ cup cocoa frosting; frost pot with remaining frosting. Pipe a band of frosting to make the pot edge with reserved cocoa frosting and petal tip #104. Repeat 2 more times over the bands to form a ridge.

Shake coconut and 2 drops green liquid food color in tightly covered jar until evenly tinted. Reserve ¼ cup green frosting; frost the grass piece with remaining frosting. Sprinkle with tinted coconut. Stack the butterscotch pieces above the pot. Pipe shamrock stems at random on cake top with reserved green frosting and writing tip #4. Pipe four dots of frosting at one end of each stem. Place the green candies on the frosting dots to form shamrocks.

TIME-SAVER TIP: Substitute 1 package (18.25 ounces) yellow cake mix with pudding for the Applesauce Cake. Prepare and bake as directed on package.

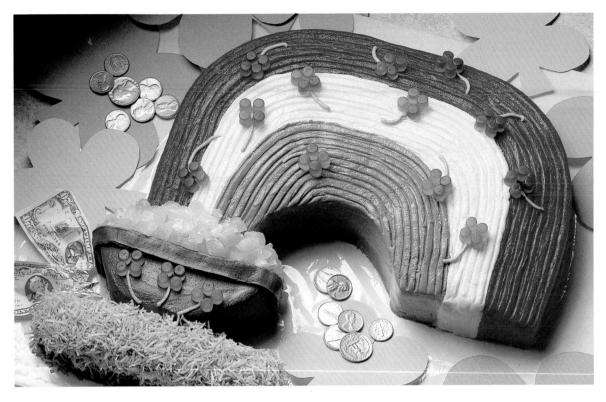

Pot-o'-Gold Cake

CUTTING AND ASSEMBLING POT-O'-GOLD CAKE

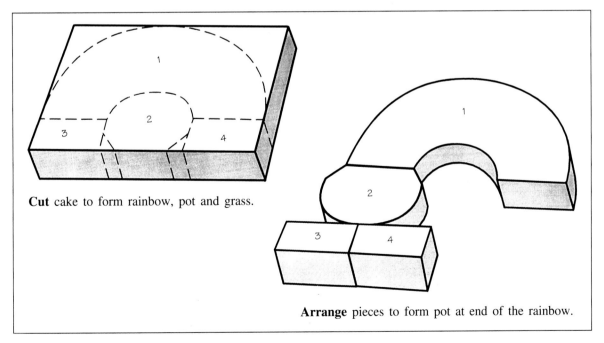

Cut cake to form rainbow, pot and grass.

Arrange pieces to form pot at end of the rainbow.

Firecracker Cakes

Chocolate-Cherry Cake (page 147)
Creamy Vanilla Frosting (page 151)
Red food color
About 12 blue birthday candles

Bake Chocolate-Cherry Cake as directed for cupcakes. Prepare Creamy Vanilla Frosting. Tint 2 cups frosting with 6 drops food color. Put 2 cupcakes together end-to-end with small amount red frosting. Frost sides of firecrackers with red frosting. Frost ends with white frosting. Insert a birthday candle in one end of each firecracker to resemble wick.

TIME-SAVER TIP: Substitute 1 package (18.25 ounces) devil's food cake mix with pudding for the Chocolate-Cherry Cake. Prepare and bake as directed on package. Substitute 1½ tubs (16 ounces each) vanilla ready-to-spread frosting for the Creamy Vanilla Frosting.

PRESIDENT'S DAY DESIGNS

Gumdrop Hatchets and Cherry Branches: For each hatchet, roll 1 large red gumdrop on heavily sugared surface into oval ⅛ inch thick. Cut hatchet as shown. Prepare Mini Bûche de Nöel Cakes (page 55). Substitute Gumdrop Hatchets for Gundrop Holly.

Firecracker Cakes

Jack-o'-Lantern Cake

Jack-o'-Lantern Cake

Make a face on the other side of the jack-o'-lantern with candy corn and shoestring licorice, or pipe on chocolate or black frosting.

> *Pumpkin-Gingerbread Cake (page 148)*
>
> *Creamy White Frosting (page 151)*
>
> *Red and yellow food colors*
>
> *Tray or cardboard, 10 inches round, covered*
>
> *1 green flat-bottom ice-cream cone*
>
> *1 teaspoon sugar*
>
> *10 large black gumdrops or 1 milk chocolate candy bar (1.55 ounces)*
>
> *1 tube (.68 ounce) green decorating gel, if desired*
>
> *Spearmint leaves, if desired*

Bake Pumpkin-Gingerbread Cake as directed for two 1½-quart casseroles. Prepare Creamy White Frosting. Tint with 6 drops each red and yellow food colors.

Trim tops of layers to make flat if necessary. Place 1 layer, rounded side down, on tray. Spread with ⅓ cup frosting. Place remaining layer, rounded side up, on top to make pumpkin. Frost with orange frosting. Make vertical lines over cake with knife to shape pumpkin. Trim cone to desired height for stem; place upside down on cake.

Sprinkle 1 teaspoon sugar on piece of waxed paper. Place gumdrops about ¼ inch apart on sugar. Top with another piece of waxed paper. Roll gumdrops between waxed paper to ¼-inch thickness. Cut eyes, nose and mouth. Arrange on pumpkin for face. Or cut candy bar into two large triangles for eyes and 7 small triangles for nose and mouth. Arrange on pumpkin for face. Decorate as desired with vines and leaves.

TIME-SAVER TIP: Substitute 2 tubs (16 ounces each) vanilla ready-to-spread frosting for the Creamy White Frosting.

Black Cat Cake

Dark Cocoa Cake (page 147)

Creamy Cocoa Frosting (page 151)

Tray or cardboard, 18 × 12 inches, covered

1 large yellow gumdrop

1 small black gumdrop

Black shoestring licorice

Bake Dark Cocoa Cake as directed for 8- or 9-inch rounds. Cut 1 layer as shown in diagram. Freeze cut pieces uncovered about 1 hour for easier frosting if desired. Prepare Creamy Cocoa Frosting. Arrange uncut layer and the pieces on tray to form cat as shown in diagram.

Frost cake, attaching pieces with small amount of frosting. Cut slice off bottom of each yellow gumdrop; use slices for eyes. Use black gumdrop for nose and shoestring licorice for whiskers and lines on eyes and front paws.

TIME-SAVER TIP: Substitute 1 package (18.25 ounces) devil's food cake mix with pudding for the Dark Cocoa Cake. Prepare and bake as directed on package. Substitute 1½ tubs (16 ounces each) chocolate ready-to-spread frosting for the Creamy Chocolate Frosting.

CUTTING AND ASSEMBLING BLACK CAT CAKE

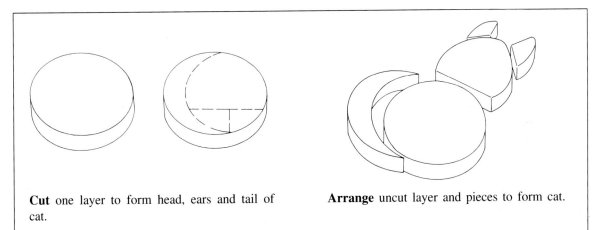

Cut one layer to form head, ears and tail of cat.

Arrange uncut layer and pieces to form cat.

Black Cat Cake

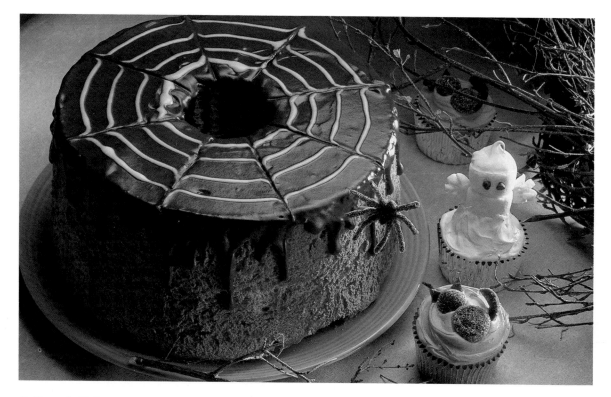

Spiderweb Cake

Spiderweb Cake

For a Christmas cake, substitute red- or green-tinted White Chocolate Glaze (page 153) for the Chocolate Glaze and top with Gumdrop Hollies (page 55).

>*Chocolate Angel Food Cake (page 145)*
>
>*Chocolate Glaze (page 153)*
>
>*¼ cup powdered sugar*
>
>*1 to 2 teaspoons hot water*
>
>*Gumdrop Spider (page right)*

Bake Chocolate Angel Food Cake as directed. Spread with Chocolate Glaze, letting glaze run down side unevenly. Mix powdered sugar and water until smooth and of drizzling consistency. Using a teaspoon and turning the plate as you work, drizzle white glaze in circles, beginning with small circle in center and encircling with larger rings ½ inch apart. Immediately draw a knife from the center outward 8 times, equally spaced, dividing into 8 equal parts (see page 00). Pin Gumdrop Spider to cake with toothpick.

TIME-SAVER TIP: Substitute 1 package (16 ounces) white angel food cake mix for the Chocolate Angel Food Cake. Prepare and bake as directed on package, except add 2 tablespoons cocoa to dry mix.

HALLOWEEN HAUNTERS

These Halloween "tricks" make cakes and cupcakes irresistable!

Gumdrop Spider: For each spider, roll 1 large black gumdrop on heavily sugared surface into oval ⅛ inch thick. Cut into desired spider shape. Place on cake or cupcakes with Web design.

Marshmallow Ghosts: For each ghost, cut 1 large marshmallow in half, crosswise. Attach 1 marshmallow half cut side down to top of whole marshmallow with a small amount of White Mountain Frosting (page 152) to form head. (Use other half of marshmallow for another ghost.) Press 2 chocolate chips into head for eyes. Make 4 small cuts in each of 2 miniature marshmallows to form fingers; flatten slightly. Attach hands to ghost with frosting. Arrange ghosts on top of cake frosted with White Mountain Frosting, bringing frosting up around bottoms so ghosts appear to be coming from frosting. Dab a small amount of frosting on top of ghosts.

Gumdrop Cat: For each cat, cut a large black gumdrop into 3 pieces as shown. Use small rounded top piece for head and largest bottom piece for body. Cut tail and ears from middle piece. Arrange to form cat.

Web Design: Drizzle round frosted or glazed cake with melted chocolate, beginning with small circle in center and encircling with larger circle, ½ inch outside the other. Immediately draw a knife from center outward 8 times, equally spaced.

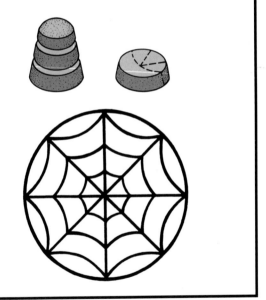

Turkey Gobbler Cake

Yellow Cake (page 150)
Fluffy Brown Sugar Frosting (page 152)
Chocolate Decorator Frosting (page 150)
Blue, yellow and orange sugars
1 gummy worm candy
Candy corn
1 chocolate chip

Bake Yellow Cake as directed for two 9-inch rounds. Cut 1 layer as shown in diagram. Freeze cut pieces uncovered about 1 hour for easier frosting. Prepare Fluffy Brown Sugar Frosting.

Place uncut layer on cake plate; frost top and side. Place circle on larger layer, ½ inch from bottom edge; frost. Arrange head and shoulders on circle; frost. Prepare Chocolate Decorator Frosting. Dip fork into chocolate frosting and lightly drag through Brown Sugar Frosting to form feathers around both layers and on shoulders.

Sprinkle blue sugar on head, yellow sugar on edge of small layer and orange sugar on edge of larger layer. Cut gummy worm in half. Place 1 candy corn on head for beak. Use gummy worm for turkey's wattle. Use chocolate chip for eye. Use candy corn for claws and feathers.

TIME-SAVER TIP: Substitute 1 package (18.25 ounces) yellow cake mix with pudding for the Yellow Cake. Prepare and bake as directed on package. Substitute 1½ tubs (16 ounces each) vanilla ready-to-spread frosting for the Creamy Vanilla Frosting and ½ tub (16-ounce size) chocolate ready-to-spread frosting for the Chocolate Decorator Frosting.

CUTTING AND ASSEMBLING TURKEY GOBBLER CAKE

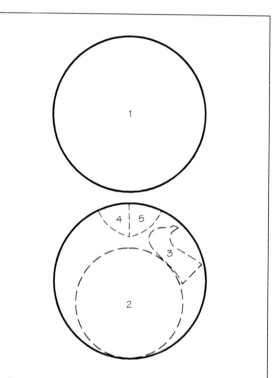

Cut one layer to form body, head and shoulders.

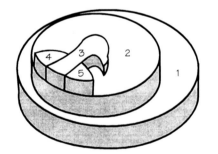

Place uncut layer on plate for tail feathers; frost. Place piece 2 on top; frost. Arrange head and shoulders on body.

Turkey Gobbler Cake and Thanksgiving Cake (page 78)

Thanksgiving Cake

When buying the fruit-shaped candies for the Cornucopia Garnishes, pick up an ounce or two more to sprinkle around the base of the cake.

Apple Cake (page 146)

Cream Cheese Frosting (page 151)

1 tablespoon cocoa

Tray or cardboard, 16 × 12 inches, covered

Cornucopia Garnishes (right)

Bake Apple Cake as directed for 13 × 9-inch rectangle. Prepare Cream Cheese Frosting. Mix ¼ cup frosting and the cocoa. Spread a 1-inch-wide stripe of cocoa frosting, ¼ inch thick, up the inside of decorating bag with star tip #30. Place 1 cup cream cheese frosting in bag. Place cake on tray. Frost cake with remaining frosting. Pipe shell border around top and base of cake, holding bag so chocolate stripe is toward the outside.

Arrange Cornucopia Garnishes in 3 rows on top of cake, pointing tips opposite direction every other row. Sprinkle cake lightly with remaining sugar mixture from Cornucopia Garnishes if desired. Arrange additional fruit candies around bottom border if desired.

TIME-SAVER TIP: Substitute 1 package (18.25 ounces) spice cake mix with pudding for the Apple Cake. Prepare and bake as directed on package. Substitute 1½ tubs (16 ounces each) cream cheese ready-to-spread frosting for the Cream Cheese Frosting.

CORNUCOPIA GARNISHES

Mix 2 tablespoons sugar and ¼ teaspoon ground cinnamon in plastic bag; reserve. Drizzle 1 teaspoon melted margarine over 12 horn-shaped corn snacks, stirring until well coated. Toss corn snacks in sugar mixture. Just before serving, place cornucopias on cake. Arrange about 5 ounces small fruit-shaped candies at openings of cornucopias for fruit spilling out. (See photo of Thanksgiving Cake on page 77).

CHOCOLATE LEAVES

Wash and dry 12 to 18 fresh nonpoisonous (unsprayed) leaves (such as lemon, grape or rose leaves) or pliable plastic leaves. Melt 2 ounces white chocolate (white baking bar), ½ cup (3 ounces) semisweet chocolate chips or 2 squares (1 ounce each) semisweet chocolate and 1 teaspoon shortening. Brush chocolate about ⅛ inch thick over backs of leaves using small brush. Refrigerate until firm, at least 1 hour. Peel off leaves, handling as little as possible. Refrigerate chocolate leaves until ready to use. (See photo of Chocolate Heart Cake on page 61.)

Two-tone Chocolate Leaves: Melt ½ cup butterscotch-flavored chips and 1 teaspoon shortening. Drizzle on the backs of leaves with a spoon; let dry. Brush melted chocolate as directed above evenly over butterscotch, completely covering backs of leaves. (See pages 142 and 143 for chocolate tips.)

Fluffy Fall Angel Food Cake

Spicy Angel Food Cake (page 145)

1½ cups whipping (heavy) cream

⅓ cup packed brown sugar

1 teaspoon vanilla

½ teaspoon pumpkin pie spice

Two-tone Chocolate Leaves (page 78)

Orange peel

Bake Spicy Angel Food Cake as directed. Beat whipping cream, brown sugar, vanilla and pumpkin pie spice in chilled bowl until stiff. Frost side and top of cake. Refrigerate until serving time.

Garnish with Two-tone Chocolate Leaves and orange peel just before serving. Refrigerate any remaining cake.

TIME-SAVER TIP: Substitute 1 package (16 ounces) white angel food cake mix for the Spicy Angel Food Cake. Prepare and bake as directed on package—except add 1 teaspoon pumpkin pie spice during last 30 seconds of beating.

Fluffy Fall Angel Food Cake

Hanukkah Dreidel Cake

Spinning the dreidel is a traditional Hanukkah game. This fun cake, made in the shape of a dreidel, will be a delightful addition to your celebration of the Jewish Festival of Lights.

Hazelnut Cake (page 149)

Creamy White Frosting (page 151)

Blue food color

1 teaspoon cocoa

Tray or cardboard, 20 × 12 inches, covered

About ½ cup miniature chocolate chips

Bake Hazelnut Cake as directed for 13 × 9-inch rectangle. Cut cake as shown in diagram. Freeze cut pieces uncovered about 1 hour for easier frosting if desired. Prepare Creamy White Frosting. Tint one-half of the frosting with 8 drops food color. Mix cocoa and ¼ cup of the white frosting.

Arrange pieces on tray to form dreidel as shown in diagram. Reserve ⅔ cup white frosting; frost the center and sides of the dreidel with remaining frosting. Reserve ⅔ cup blue frosting; frost the driedel point, handle top and sides with the remaining frosting, attaching pieces with small amount of frosting. Outline the Hebrew letter of your choice with a toothpick. Fill in with cocoa frosting; outline with chocolate chips.

Place reserved white frosting in decorating bag with star tip #32. Pipe a shell border along base and top edge of white-frosted cake. Pipe a shell border along base and top edge of blue-frosted cake with blue frosting and shell tip. Outline top borders with chocolate chips if desired.

TIME-SAVER TIP: Substitute 1 package (18.25 ounces) white cake mix with pudding for the Hazelnut Cake. Prepare and bake as directed on package. Substitute 2 tubs (16 ounces each) vanilla ready-to-spread frosting for the Creamy White Frosting.

CUTTING AND ASSEMBLING HANUKKAH DREIDEL CAKE

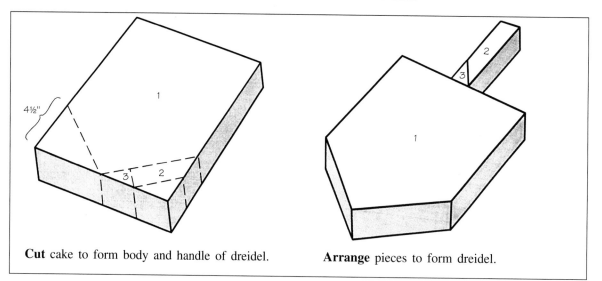

Cut cake to form body and handle of dreidel.

Arrange pieces to form dreidel.

Hanukkah Dreidel Cake

3

Celebration Cakes

Classic White Wedding Cake (page 84)

Classic White Wedding Cake

For the entire wedding cake, prepare 6 recipes White Cake, 2 recipes Creamy White Frosting, using clear vanilla, and as many recipes White Decorator Frosting, using clear vanilla, as necessary. Prepare batter just before baking; measure ingredients ahead if desired. Bake cake layers the day before they are to be assembled, or bake them earlier and freeze.

White Cake (page 149)

Creamy White Frosting (page 151)

Large tray, mirror or aluminum-foil covered cardboard, 16 inches round

Aluminum foil-covered cardboard, 10 inches round

Aluminum foil-covered cardboard, 6 inches round

White Decorator Frosting (page 153)

Grease and flour 1 round pan, 10 × 2 inches. Prepare 1 recipe White Cake. Pour 4½ cups batter into pan. Bake 45 to 50 minutes or until top springs back when touched lightly in center. Cool 15 minutes; remove from pan. Cool completely.

Grease and flour 1 round pan, 14 × 2 inches, and 1 round pan, 6 × 2 inches. Prepare 2 recipes White Cake, 1 recipe at a time. Pour 1½ cups batter into 6-inch pan and 7¾ cups batter into 14-inch pan. Bake 6-inch layer 35 to 40 minutes, 14-inch layer 50 to 55 minutes or until top springs back when touched lightly in center. Cool 15 minutes; remove from pans. Cool completely.

Repeat above process, making a total of 6 layers. Each tier of wedding cake will consist of 2 layers. (Height must measure 3 inches total or 1½ inches per layer.) Tops of layers should be flat for ease in stacking. Slice off rounded tops if necessary.

Prepare 1 recipe Creamy White Frosting. Place one 14-inch layer on tray. Fill and frost 14-inch tier, using 1 cup frosting to fill and remaining to frost. Place covered 10-inch cardboard circle on first tier; place 10-inch layer on cardboard.

Prepare 1 recipe Creamy White Frosting. Fill and frost 10-inch tier, using ¾ cup frosting to fill and 2 cups to frost. Place covered 6-inch cardboard circle on second tier; place 6-inch layer on cardboard. Fill and frost 6-inch tier, using ⅓ cup frosting to fill and remaining to frost.

Prepare White Decorator Frosting, 1 recipe at a time. Place in decorating bag with petal tip #103. Make desired number of roses (see page 142); refrigerate until ready to use. Pipe shell border around top edge and base of each tier with open star tip #18. Arrange roses on cake as desired. Pipe vines with writing tip #4 and leaves with leaf tip #352 onto roses. Top with fresh flowers if desired (see Fresh Flower Decorations on page 88).

HOW TO CUT A WEDDING CAKE

Use a thin, sharp or serrated knife. Insert knife into cake, keeping point down and handle up. Slice, pulling knife toward you. If frosting sticks, dip knife in hot water or wipe with damp paper towel after cutting each slice.

Round Tiered Cake

Cut vertically through bottom layer at edge of second layer as indicated by dotted line 1; then cut into wedges as indicated by dotted line 2.

Follow same procedure with middle layer by cutting vertically through second layer at edge of top layer as indicated by dotted line 3; then cut into wedges as indicated by dotted line 4.

Return to bottom layer and cut along dotted line 5; cut into wedges as indicated by dotted line 6. Separate remaining layers (traditionally the top layer is frozen for the couple's first anniversary); cut into desired sizes.

WEDDING CAKE YIELDS—SERVINGS PER 2-LAYER TIER

Each serving measures 2 × 1 inch from a tier 3 inches high.

Layer	Round	Square
6 inches	10	18
7 inches	15	—
8 inches	22	32
9 inches	28	40
10 inches	35	50
12 inches	50	72
14 inches	70	98
16 inches	100	128
18 × 12-inch rectangle		108

BAKING DIFFERENT SIZES

Layers of other sizes can be made. One recipe Silver White Cake yields about 5 cups batter.

Pan Size	Amount of Batter	Baking Time
7 × 2-inch round	2 cups	40 to 45 minutes
9 × 2-inch round	3 cups	40 to 45 minutes
10 × 2-inch round	4½ cups	45 to 50 minutes
12 × 2-inch round	5 cups	45 to 50 minutes

Apricot-Almond Wedding Cake

For the entire wedding cake, prepare 3 recipes Almond Cake and 2 recipes Creamy White Frosting, using almond extract. Edible glitter is available at specialty cake decorating stores. Prepare batter just before baking; measure ingredients ahead if desired. Bake cake layers the day before they are to be assembled, or bake them earlier and freeze.

> *Almond Cake (page 149)*
>
> *2 packages (6 ounces each) premier white baking bars*
>
> *Creamy White Frosting (page 151)*
>
> *Red and yellow food colors*
>
> *Large tray, mirror or aluminum foil-covered cardboard, 14 inches round*
>
> *1¼ cups apricot fruit spread*
>
> *Aluminum foil-covered cardboard, 9 inches round*
>
> *White edible glitter, if desired*

Grease and flour 2 round pans, 9 × 1½ inches. Prepare 1 recipe Almond Cake. Pour into pans. Bake 30 to 35 minutes or until top springs back when touched lightly in center. Cool 15 minutes; remove from pan. Cool completely.

Grease and flour 1 round pan, 12 × 2 inches. Prepare 1 recipe Almond Cake. Pour into pan. Bake 45 to 50 minutes or until top springs back when touched lightly in center. Cool 15 minutes; remove from pan. Cool completely. Repeat.

Each tier of wedding cake will consist of 2 layers. Tops of layers should be flat for ease in stacking. Slice off rounded tops if necessary.

Prepare white chocolate ribbons, using white baking bars, as directed for Chocolate Ribbons (page 144). Place ribbons on cookie sheet; set aside. (It is important that these be prepared before frosting the cake because they will not adhere to frosting once it is set.)

Prepare 1 recipe Creamy White Frosting. Tint with 2 drops red and 6 drops yellow food color. Place one 12-inch layer on tray. Spread ¾ cup fruit spread evenly over layer. Top with remaining 12-inch layer. Frost 12-inch tier. Place 9-inch cardboard circle on first tier.

Prepare 1 recipe Creamy White Frosting. Tint with 2 drops red and 6 drops yellow food color. Place one 9-inch layer on cardboard. Spread ½ cup fruit spread evenly over layer. Top with remaining layer. Frost 9-inch tier. Gently press ribbons into side and top of tier. Sprinkle with white edible glitter. Decorate with Chocolate Leaves (page 78) and Chocolate Twigs (page 144) made from white chocolate and Apricot Roses (page 88) if desired.

CAKES IN BLOOM

Spring time, or any time, add the elegance and simplicity of flowers to your cakes with these fresh flower ideas and beautifully crafted look-alikes.

Gumdrop Rose: Roll 4 large red gumdrops on well-sugared surface into ovals ⅛ inch thick as shown. Sprinkle with sugar. Cut ovals into halves. Roll 1 half-oval tightly to form center of rose. Place more half-ovals around center, overlapping slightly. Press together at base; trim base. Roll out green gumdrops to cut leaves if desired.

Apricot Rose: Follow directions above for Gumdrop Rose, except use dried apricot halves.

Fresh Flower Decorations: Fresh edible flowers can enhance the attractiveness of a cake. Select fresh flowers that can last out of water for several hours without wilting. Or, insert ends of flowers in watering tubes. But-tercups, carnations, chrysanthemums, daisies, pansies, roses and violets are all good choices. Request unsprayed flowers when ordering. If you think flowers may have been sprayed with a pesticide, dip them in soapy water, rinse and dry before placing on cake. A small piece of plastic wrap also can be placed beneath the flowers that will touch the cake. Accent with baby's breath or greenery such as ferns. (See photo of Classic White Wedding Cake on page 82.)

Sugared Roses: Dip small fresh roses in water, rinse and pat dry. Trim stems to about 2 inches. Mix 2 tablespoons light corn syrup and 1 teaspoon water. Brush mixture on rose petals with small, soft brush, separating petals as you coat them. Sift or sprinkle superfine or granulated sugar lightly on roses, shaking gently to remove excess sugar. Other flowers that can be sugared are bachelor buttons, carnations, chrysanthemums, small orchids, sweet peas and violets. Do not eat flowers. (See photo of Chocolate Heart Cake on page 62.)

Whipped Cream Rosettes: Whip 1 cup whipping cream and 2 tablespoons powdered sugar. Pipe rosettes (see page 138) onto wax paper–lined cookie sheet. Freeze until firm; carefully remove from waxed paper. Wrap and store in freezer. Use to decorate cakes that will be cut and served or place on individual serving as they are cut.

Frosted Grapes: Dip small clusters of grapes into water, then into superfine or granulated sugar. Dry clusters on wire rack before adding to cake. Champagne grapes are especially attractive this way. Whole cranberries can also be frosted.

Petits Fours

White Cake (page 149)
Petits Fours Glaze (page 153)
2 cups powdered sugar
2 to 3 tablespoons water

Bake White Cake as directed for jelly roll pan. Cut cake into 1½-inch squares, rounds, diamonds or hearts.

Place cakes, one at a time, on wire rack over large bowl. Pour enough Petits Fours Glaze over top to cover top and sides. (Glaze can be reheated and used again.)

Mix powdered sugar and just enough water to make a frosting that holds its shape. Place frosting in decorating bag with writing tip #3. Decorate as desired. *About 54 pieces.*

Petits Fours

Anniversary Cake

This pretty and unusual cake will also be perfect for showers, birthdays and as a small wedding cake.

Pastel Marble Cake (page 149)
Buttercream Frosting (page 150)

Bake Pastel Marble Cake as directed for 13 × 9-inch rectangle. Prepare Buttercream Frosting; reserve 3½ cups. Frost cake with remaining frosting. Mark a 2-inch border around top edge of cake. Place ⅔ cup at a time of the reserved frosting in decorating bag with star tip #18. Pipe diagonal lines inside border; repeat at opposite diagonal. Pipe shell borders around top and bottom edges of cake and inside border.

Pipe message in center of cake. Decorate with Fresh Flower Decorations (page 88) if desired.

TIME-SAVER TIP: Substitute 1 package (18.25 ounces) white cake mix with pudding for the Pastel Marble Cake. Prepare and bake as directed on package—except tint batter and spoon into pan as directed in recipe.

MARSHMALLOW FLOWERS

For every 3 flowers, snip 3 pink miniature marshmallows into thirds, making sure not to cut entirely through marshmallows. Fan marshmallow pieces out. Snip 1 green miniature marshmallow into 3 pieces. Attach 1 green piece to each pink flower by pressing gently in place. Press a silver nonpareil in center of each flower. (Spray hands and scissors with nonstick vegetable cooking spray to keep marshmallows from sticking.) Remove silver nonpariels before eating.

Double-ring Shower Cake

This double-ring cake does double (or even triple) duty! Use it for wedding showers, anniversaries or as a small wedding cake.

2 recipes Almond Cake (page 149)
32 Marshmallow Flowers (left)
Creamy White Frosting (page 151)
Red food color
Tray or cardboard, 24 × 14 inches, covered

Bake 1 recipe Almond Cake as directed for 12-cup ring mold; repeat. Prepare Marshmallow Flowers; set aside.

Prepare Creamy White Frosting. Tint ½ cup with 2 drops food color; reserve. Cut cake as shown in diagram. Arrange pieces on tray to form double-ring as shown in diagram. Frost cake, attaching pieces with small amount of frosting.

Place reserved pink frosting in decorating bag with star tip #18. Pipe shell border around outside and inside base of rings. Mark half circles around upper outside edge of cake rings with 2-inch diameter glass (or with ruler and toothpick). Pipe swag border around cake, following scalloped markings with writing tip #4. Place Marshmallow Flower where swag border touches top edge of cake. Place flowers around inside edges of rings about every 2 inches.

TIME-SAVER TIP: Substitute 2 packages (18.25 ounces each) white cake mix with pudding for the 2 recipes Almond Cake. Prepare and bake as directed for 12-cup ovenproof ring mold. Substitute 2 tubs (16 ounces each) vanilla ready-to-spread frosting for the Creamy White Frosting.

Anniversary Cake and Double-ring Shower Cake

CUTTING AND ASSEMBLING DOUBLE RING SHOWER CAKE

Cut piece from side of one ring to fit arc of second ring.

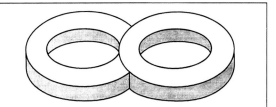

Join rings together, fitting second ring into cut section of first ring.

Umbrella Cake

Lemon–Poppy Seed Cake (page 150)

Fluffy Citrus Frosting (page 152)

Yellow food color

Tray or cardboard, 22 × 18 inches, covered

Paste candies

Ribbon, for bow

Bake Lemon–Poppy Seed Cake as directed for 2 heart pans. Cut cake as shown in diagram. Freeze uncovered about 1 hour for easier frosting if desired. Prepare Fluffy Citrus Frosting, using lemon peel; reserve 1½ cups. Tint remaining frosting with 8 drops food color. Arrange cake pieces on tray to form umbrella as shown in diagram, trimming pieces 2 and 3 for handle. Frost top of umbrella with yellow frosting and handle with white frosting, attaching pieces with small amount of frosting. Decorate with candy sequins as desired. Attach bow at handle.

TIME-SAVER TIP: Substitute 1 package (18.25 ounces) lemon cake mix with pudding for the Lemon–Poppy Seed Cake. Prepare and bake as directed for 2 heart pans. Substitute 2 packages (7.2 ounces each) fluffy white frosting mix for the Fluffy Citrus Frosting. Prepare as directed on package. Tint with yellow food color.

ALMOND FLOWERS

For each flower, place tips of 5 sliced almonds in frostings to form a flower using almonds as the petals. Pipe a drop of frosting in the center with a small star tip. Or, place small candy in center.

CUTTING AND ASSEMBLING UMBRELLA CAKE

Cut one heart cake vertically in half.

Cut a piece from each side of second heart, matching the length of the cuts.

Arrange pieces to form umbrella, trimming pieces 2 and 3 for handle.

Baby Bib Shower Cake and Bootie Shower Cakes

Baby Bib Shower Cake

Hazelnut Cake (page 149)
Creamy Vanilla Frosting (page 151)
Red and blue food colors
Pastel candy mints

Bake Hazelnut Cake as directed for two 8- or 9-inch rounds. Prepare Creamy Vanilla Frosting; reserve 1 cup. Fill and frost cake with remaining frosting. Make vertical lines on side of cake with decorating comb or tines of fork if desired.

Place ½ cup reserved frosting in decorating bag with petal tip #124. Pipe ruffle around outer top edge of cake, leaving 3-inch opening at top.

Tint two-thirds of remaining frosting with 2 drops blue food color. Pipe outer border of bib with blue frosting and writing tip #5. Pipe inner opening of bib about 3 inches in diameter; join circles with tie at top. Make small bows on bib and write desired message in bib opening. Tint remaining frosting with 2 drops of red food color; pipe dots between bows. Arrange mints around base of cake.

TIME-SAVER TIP: Substitute 1 package (18.25 ounces) white cake mix with pudding for the Hazelnut Cake. Prepare and bake as directed on package. Substitute 1½ tubs (16 ounces each) vanilla ready-to-spread frosting for the Creamy Vanilla Frosting.

Bootie Shower Cakes

Tint the booties pastel yellow, blue or pink for a traditional look or bright colors for a fun, contemporary look.

White Cake (page 149)
White Mountain Frosting (page 152)
Food colors, if desired
Striped fruit-flavored chewing gum

Bake White Cake as directed for cupcakes. Remove paper baking cups. Place 2 cupcakes upside down on separate plates. Cut small piece off side of a third cupcake to form flat surface. Cut third cupcake horizontally in half. Place one half with cut side against cupcake on plate to form bootie as shown in diagram. Place remaining half against second cupcake. Repeat with remaining cupcakes.

Prepare Fluffy White Frosting; reserve ⅔ cup. Tint remaining frosting if desired. Frost booties, attaching pieces with small amount of frosting. Place reserved frosting in decorating bag with writing tip #4. Outline top and tongue of booties with frosting. Cut chewing gum into strips for accents and laces; place on booties.

TIME-SAVER TIP: Substitute 1 package (18.25 ounces) white cake mix with pudding for the White Cake. Prepare and bake as directed on package. Substitute 2 packages (7.2 ounces each) fluffy white frosting mix for the Fluffy White Frosting. Prepare as directed on package.

CUTTING AND ASSEMBLING BOOTIE SHOWER CAKES

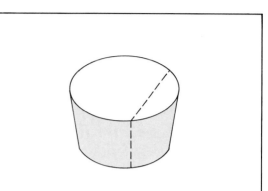

Cut piece off side of one cupcake.

Cut cupcake horizontally into halves.

Place halves with cut sides against two other cupcakes.

"Birthday-saurus" Bash Cake

Look for cookies that have opposites in the package so you can get matching "pairs" to make the front and back of each dinosaur.

16 spearmint leaves

Apple Cake (page 146)

Tray or cardboard, 16 × 2 inches, covered

Creamy White Frosting (page 151)

Red, yellow and green food colors

4 pretzel rods

6 dinosaur-shaped cookies (2 each of three different shapes)

Dinosaur-shaped candy sprinkles

Roll spearmint leaves to ⅛-inch thickness. Trim, if necessary, to retain leaf shape. Snip edges to resemble palm leaves. Quickly dip in cool water. Allow to dry on wire rack at least 24 hours to stiffen.

Bake Apple Cake as directed for 13 × 9-inch rectangle. Place cake on tray. Prepare Creamy White Frosting. Tint ¼ cup frosting with 2 drops red food color and ½ cup frosting with 3 drops yellow food color. Tint remaining frosting with 8 drops green food color.

Place pink frosting in decorating bag with writing tip #4. Pipe detail lines on fronts and backs of 1 set of dinosaur cookies. Pipe detail lines on fronts and backs of the other 2 sets of cookies with yellow frosting and writing tip. Attach 4 leaves together with small amount of green frosting.

Reserve ¾ cup green frosting; frost cake with remaining frosting. Pipe shell border around top and base of cake with reserved green frosting and star tip #32; sprinkle with dinosaur-shaped candies. Break off about 2 inches from each pretzel for tree trunks. Arrange on cake, pushing broken end of pretzel all the way through cake. Pipe stars around base of each trunk to anchor.

Write name on top of cake with yellow frosting and writing tip #4. Decorate with candy sprinkles as desired. Attach cookie sets back to back with small amount of frosting. Slide 2 flat toothpicks between the cookies at the base about 1 inch apart to serve as standing supports. Place on cake. Attach leaves to trunks with small amount of green frosting. Decorate with additional candies as desired.

TIME-SAVER TIP: Substitute 1 package (18.25 ounces) yellow cake mix with pudding for the Apple Cake. Prepare and bake as directed on package. Substitute 2 tubs (16 ounces each) vanilla ready-to-spread frosting for the Creamy White Frosting.

"Birthday-saurus" Bash Cake

STENCILS

Stencils can be cut from lightweight cardboard, waxed paper or sheets of plastic cut to the size of the cake. Or, use doilies or purchased stencils. Place stencil on unfrosted, frosted or glazed cake. (Allow frostings and glazes to set before stenciling.) Sift cocoa, powdered sugar, ground cinnamon or nutmeg, colored sugars or gelatin over stencil. Carefully remove stencil to show design. For more intricate designs, use 2 or 3 different colored ingredients. (See photo of Flower Silhouette Birthday Cake on page 99.)

Flower Silhouette Birthday Cake

Wouldn't this cake be wonderful for Mother's Day? Make your own stencil using lightweight cardboard or purchase a stencil at a craft store or paint and wallpapering store. Do not freeze the frosted cake after decorating with colored sugars, because the colors will run.

Marble Cake (page 149)

Creamy Vanilla Frosting (page 151)

Assorted colored sugars

Food color

Flower design stencil (page 97)

Bake Marble Cake as directed for two 8- or 9-inch rounds. Prepare Creamy Vanilla Frosting; reserve ¼ cup. Fill layers with about ⅓ cup remaining frosting; frost cake.

Position paper stencil with a flower design on top of cake. Sprinkle colored sugars over stencil, being careful not to mix colors or get sugar on other areas of cake surface; remove stencil. Tint reserved ¼ cup frosting with 2 drops of desired food color. Place frosting in decorating bag with writing tip #4. Pipe desired message on cake. Pipe design on edge of plate if desired.

TIME-SAVER TIP: Substitute 1 package (18.25 ounces) fudge marble cake mix with pudding for the Marble Cake. Prepare and bake as directed on package. Substitute 1½ tubs (16 ounces each) vanilla ready-to-spread frosting for the Creamy Vanilla Frosting.

Happy Birthday Cake

Any color can be used to decorate this versatile cake. For a more elegant cake, use Creamy Chocolate Frosting (page 150) and substitute chocolate and caramel candies for the fruit candies.

Orange-Coconut Cake (page 150)

Creamy Citrus Frosting (page 151)

Yellow food color

15 to 20 square candy fruit chews

Bake Orange-Coconut Cake as directed for two 8- or 9-inch rounds. Prepare Creamy Citrus Frosting, using orange juice and peel. Tint 1½ cups frosting with 3 drops food color. Fill layers and frost cake with remaining frosting.

Place yellow frosting in decorating bag with star tip #32. Pipe shell border around top and base of cake. Pipe a ribbon and bow on each candy square to resemble a wrapped package with writing tip #4. Arrange packages on top of cake.

TIME-SAVER TIP: Substitute 1 package (18.25 ounces) yellow cake mix with pudding for the Orange-Coconut Cake. Prepare and bake as directed on package. Substitute 1½ tubs (16 ounces each) vanilla ready-to-spread frosting for the Creamy Citrus Frosting.

Flower Silhouette Birthday Cake and Happy Birthday Cake

Mother's Day Straw Hat Cake

Applesauce Cake (page 145)

3 cups plus 2 tablespoons powdered sugar

¼ cup milk

3 tablespoons shortening

½ teaspoon vanilla

4 teaspoons cocoa

1 red candy-coated chocolate candy

1 round vanilla wafer cookie, about 1½ inches in diameter

Yellow, red and green food colors

Creamy White Frosting (page 00)

4 teaspoons cocoa

Bake Applesauce Cake as directed for 9-inch round and 6 × 3-inch ovenproof bowl. Beat powdered sugar, milk, shortening and vanilla on medium speed until smooth. Mix 4 teaspoons cocoa into ½ cup frosting. Reserve remaining frosting. Place cocoa frosting in decorating bag with writing tip #2. Pipe a line down center of red candy; pipe 2 small dots on each side of line to make ladybug body. Pipe a line perpendicular to the center line at one end for ladybug head; set aside.

Trace around vanilla cookie on waxed paper with a toothpick; reserve. Pipe small dots with cocoa frosting and writing tip #4 close together on cookie to cover for center of sunflower. Tint ½ cup of the reserved white frosting with 5 drops yellow food color and 1 drop red food color. Pipe a row of sunflower petals with yellow frosting and petal tip #352 around the traced circle on waxed paper, making sure to start petals on edge of circle. Repeat, staggering second row of petals inside circle and overlapping outer row. Place cookie sunflower center in center of petals on waxed paper. Set aside to dry.

Prepare Creamy White Frosting; reserve ¼ cup. Tint remaining tan with 4 teaspoons cocoa and 10 drops yellow food color. Place cake layer on cake plate. Frost side with tan frosting; frost top with thin layer. Trim top of bowl cake to make flat if necessary. Place upside down in center of layer. Frost with thin layer tan frosting. Place ⅔ cup tan frosting at a time in decorating bag with ribbon tip #47. Pipe a line of frosting from base of the dome, up and over to the base on the other side, dividing cake in half. Starting at the center top on either side of the piped line, continue making lines from the top to the base until there are 16 "spokes." Starting about 1 inch from top of cake, pipe over every other spoke, alternating rows to achieve a woven look.

On the brim, at the dome base, pipe a spoke out to the cake edge in the shape of a backwards J. Pipe a small U shape at the edge, starting where the J begins to bend following around the curve. Repeat these two steps, making an even number of spokes and curved edges, spacing them about ½ inch apart. Starting again at the dome base, pipe over every other spoke, working out to the cake edge.

Place ½ cup of the white frosting in a decorating bag with petal tip #104. Pipe strip of frosting around base of the dome for hatband. Repeat for a second layer. Pipe about 1 tablespoon white frosting on hatband where sunflower is to be placed. Carefully remove sunflower from waxed paper; place on hatband.

Mix remaining reserved white frosting and 3 drops green food color. Pipe leaves around sunflower with green frosting and leaf tip #352, starting under petals when possible. Pipe 3 white flowers on leaves with petal tip #190. Place ladybug on a leaf. Pipe centers on white flowers with yellow frosting and writing tip #4.

Mother's Day Straw Hat Cake

PIPING BRIM OF HAT

On the brim, at the dome base, pipe a spoke out to the cake edge, making a backwards *J*. Pipe a small *u* shape at the edge; repeat.

Father's Day T-Shirt Cake

Father's Day T-Shirt Cake

Don't stop at Father's Day; this cake would be great for Dad's birthday, too! Or change the message and use for any sports enthusiast.

> *Hazelnut Cake (page 149)*
>
> *Creamy White Frosting (page 151)*
>
> *1 tablespoon cocoa*
>
> *Tray or cardboard, 16 × 14 inches, covered*
>
> *Yellow sugar*

Bake Hazelnut Cake as directed for 13 × 9-inch rectangle. Cut cake as shown in diagram. Freeze cut pieces uncovered about 1 hour for easier frosting if desired. Prepare Creamy White Frosting; reserve 1 cup. Stir cocoa into ½ cup of frosting; reserve.

Arrange cake pieces on tray to form T-shirt as shown in diagram. Frost with white frosting, attaching sleeve with small amount of frosting. Trace lettering pattern on waxed paper. Place on top of cake and poke small holes about ¼ inch apart on tracing lines to outline lettering. Remove waxed paper. Place cocoa frosting in decorating bag with writing tip #4. Pipe over outline of lettering. Pipe stitching lines for sleeves, hem and neck ribbing. Fill in lettering with yellow sugar. Place reserved 1 cup white frosting in decorating bag with star tip #32. Pipe shell border around base of cake; sprinkle with yellow sugar.

TIME-SAVER TIP: Substitute 1 package (18.25 ounces) white cake mix with pudding for the Hazelnut Cake. Prepare and bake as directed on package. Substitute 2 tubs (16 ounces each) vanilla ready-to-spread frosting for the Creamy White Frosting.

CUTTING AND ASSEMBLING FATHER'S DAY T-SHIRT CAKE

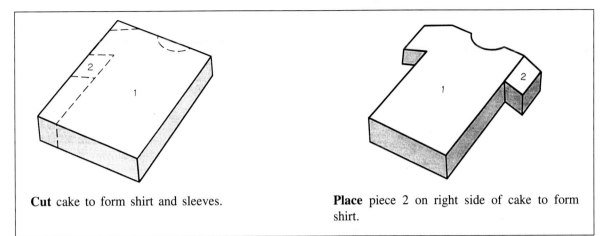

Cut cake to form shirt and sleeves.

Place piece 2 on right side of cake to form shirt.

PIPING SCRIPT

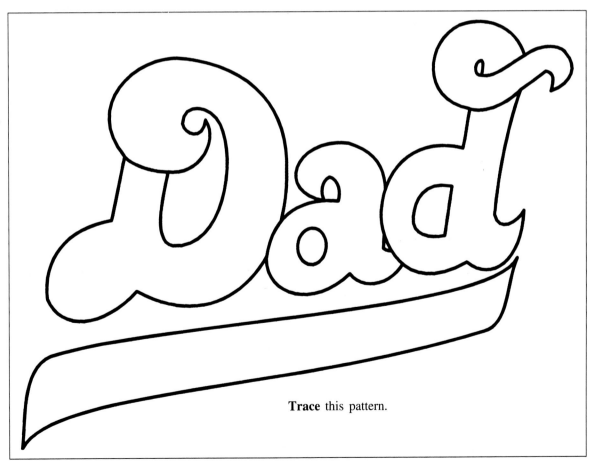

Trace this pattern.

Computer Cake

Celebrate a graduation, new job, promotion or birthday in the computer age!

2 recipes Applesauce Cake (page 145)

Creamy Vanilla Frosting (page 151)

Tray or cardboard, 19 × 14 inches, covered

Blue food color

Red and black shoestring licorice

39 whole almonds

Chocolate chips

Bake 2 recipes Applesauce Cake as directed for 13 × 9-inch rectangle. Cut cake as shown in diagram. Freeze pieces uncovered about 1 hour for easier frosting if desired. Prepare Creamy Vanilla Frosting; reserve ¾ cup. Arrange cake pieces on tray to form computer as shown in diagram. Frost cake, attaching pieces with small amount of frosting.

Drop 1 drop food color about 3 inches in from each corner of the screen area. Blend into frosting with spatula to within 1 inch of edges to make screen. Outline with licorice. Arrange almonds on keyboard in 5 rows of 6 and a bottom row of 9. Trim mouse to desired shape. Frost with ½ cup of reserved frosting. Place mouse on keyboard; attach to computer with licorice. Outline mouse key with toothpick or use a piece of white chocolate. Place remaining frosting in decorating bag with writing tip #4. Write desired message on screen. Decorate screen with chocolate chips.

TIME-SAVER TIP: Substitute 2 packages (18.25 ounces) yellow cake mix with pudding for the Applesauce Cake. Prepare and bake as directed on package. Substitute 1½ tubs (16 ounces each) vanilla ready-to-spread frosting for the Creamy Vanilla Frosting.

CUTTING AND ASSEMBLING COMPUTER CAKE

Cut diagonal pieces from both sides of one rectangle; cut mouse.

Arrange uncut rectangle on top of cut rectangle to form keyboard and screen.

Computer Cake

Gone Fishin' Cake

Buttermilk Spice Cake (page 146)
Tray or cardboard, 18 × 13 inches, covered
Creamy Vanilla Frosting (page 151)
Blue food color
¼ cup cocoa
1 candy stick (5 inches)
1 ring-shaped hard candy
2-inch fish-shaped cookie cutter
Colored sugar
5 gummy fish candies

Bake Buttermilk Spice Cake as directed for 15½ × 10½ × 1-inch jelly roll. Place on tray. Prepare Creamy Vanilla Frosting. Reserve ⅔ cup for decorating. Frost cake with remaining frosting, making top smooth. Place 1 drop food color on tip of spatula. Pat color in several places along bottom of cake; swirl into frosting for water.

Sift cocoa over reserved frosting; stir until smooth, adding 1 to 2 teaspoons water if necessary. Place cocoa frosting in decorating bag with writing tip #2. Write desired ''gone fishing'' message on cake. Place candy stick and ring-shaped hard candy on top of cake to form fishing rod and reel. Pipe on fishing line with cocoa frosting. Place fish-shaped cookie cutter on cake at end of fishing line; sprinkle colored sugar inside cutter, pressing gently into frosting. Carefully remove cookie cutter. Or, place a frog-shaped candy at end of fish line for bait.

Pipe stringer on cake with cocoa frosting. Arrange gummy fish around stringer. Pipe shell border around top edge and base of cake with cocoa frosting and star tip #18.

TIME-SAVER TIP: Substitute 1 package (18.25 ounces) yellow or spice cake mix with pudding for the Buttermilk Spice Cake. Prepare and bake as directed on package.

Housewarming Cake

Whole Wheat Applesauce Cake (page 145)
Tray or cardboard, 16 × 12 inches, covered
Creamy Vanilla Frosting (page 151)
Black shoestring licorice
Vanilla wafer cookies
Green candy sprinkles
Yellow candy fruit slice
3 cylinder licorice candies
½ large orange gumdrop
Green rock candy
Yellow food color

Bake Whole Wheat Applesauce Cake as directed for 13 × 9-inch rectangle. Place on tray. Prepare Creamy Vanilla Frosting; reserve 2 tablespoons. Frost cake with remaining frosting. Outline door and make bricks with a toothpick or knife.

Outline door frame with shoestring licorice. Attach wafers at base of door for stoop. Use green sprinkles for grass, fruit slice for window, licorice cylinders for hinges and door handle, gumdrop for planter and rock candy for plant. Add flowers as desired.

Tint reserved frosting with 5 drops of food color. Place in decorating bag with writing tip #4. Pipe on house number and mailbox. Write new neighbor's name with decorating gel.

TIME-SAVER TIP: Substitute 1 package (18.25 ounces) yellow or spice cake mix with pudding for the Whole Wheat Applesauce Cake. Prepare and bake as directed on package.

Gone Fishin' Cake and Housewarming Cake

Star of David Cake

Bar and Bat Mitzvahs, a trip to Israel and Hebrew school parties are all wonderful occasions for this cake.

White Cake (page 149)

Creamy White Frosting (page 151)

Tray or cardboard, 14 × 14 inches, covered

Food color

Colored sugar

Bake White Cake as directed for 13 × 9-inch rectangle. Cut cake as shown in diagram. Freeze cut pieces uncovered about 1 hour for easier frosting if desired. Prepare Creamy White Frosting; reserve 1½ cups.

Arrange cake pieces on tray to form star as shown in diagram, attaching pieces with small amount of frosting. Frost cake with remaining white frosting. Place ½ cup of the reserved frosting in decorating bag with star tip #32. Pipe shell border around base of cake. Tint remaining reserved frosting with desired food color. Pipe 3 rows of stars with star tip #32 around top edge of cake, starting and stopping so that triangles appear interwoven. Sprinkle frosted top of cake lightly with sugar; sprinkle on border if desired.

TIME-SAVER TIP: Substitute 1 package (18.25 ounces) white cake mix with pudding for the White Cake. Prepare and bake as directed on package. Substitute 2 tubs (16 ounces each) vanilla ready-to-spread frosting for the Creamy White Frosting.

CUTTING AND ASSEMBLING STAR OF DAVID CAKE

Cut cake to form one large triangle and three smaller ones.

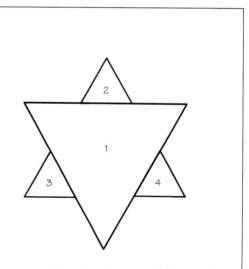

Arrange smaller triangles around large triangle to complete star points.

Star of David Cake

4

Specialty Bakery Cakes

Custard-filled Nutmeg Cake
French Silk Filbert Cake
Caramel-Pecan Torte
Chocolate Cookie Cake
Decadent Chocolate Cake with Rapsberry Sauce
Maple-Pecan Cake

Strawberries with Cream Cake
Lemon Meringue Cake
Mocha Cream Torte
Walnut Torte
Marzipan Torte
Chocolate Mint Loaves

Custard-filled Nutmeg Cake (page 112) and French Silk Filbert Cake (page 113)

Custard-filled Nutmeg Cake

Nutmeg Cake (below)

Custard Cream Filling (below)

Powdered sugar

Stencil or paper doily

Strawberries

Green grape clusters

Mint leaves

Bake Nutmeg Cake as directed. Prepare Custard Cream Filling. Split cake horizontally to make 4 layers (see page 132). Fill each layer with one-third of the filling. Place stencil on top layer; press powdered sugar generously through sieve over stencil. Carefully remove stencil. Apply second layer of stenciling using ground nutmeg if desired. Garnish base of cake with strawberries, grapes and mint leaves. Refrigerate any remaining cake. *16 servings.*

NUTMEG CAKE

2 cups plus 2 tablespoons all-purpose flour

1½ cups sugar

½ cup shortening

1 cup milk

3½ teaspoons baking powder

1 teaspoon salt

1 teaspoon ground nutmeg

1 teaspoon vanilla

3 eggs

Heat oven to 350°. Grease and flour 2 round pans, 9 × 1½ inches. Beat all ingredients in large bowl on medium speed 30 seconds, scraping bowl constantly. Beat on high speed 3 minutes, scraping bowl occasionally. Pour batter into pans.

Bake 30 to 35 minutes or until toothpick inserted in center comes out clean. Cool 10 minutes; remove from pans. Cool completely.

CUSTARD CREAM FILLING

⅔ cup sugar

4 tablespoons cornstarch

¼ teaspoon salt

3 cups milk

4 egg yolks, slightly beaten

1½ teaspoons vanilla

Mix sugar, cornstarch and salt in 2-quart saucepan. Stir in milk gradually. Cook over medium heat, stirring constantly, until mixture thickens and boils. Boil and stir 1 minute. Stir about half of the hot mixture gradually into egg yolks. Blend into hot mixture in saucepan. Boil and stir 1 minute; remove from heat. Stir in vanilla; cool.

TIME-SAVER TIP: Substitute 1 package (18.25 ounces) yellow cake mix with pudding for the Nutmeg Cake. Prepare and bake as directed on package—except add 1 teaspoon ground nutmeg before beating.

French Silk Filbert Cake

White Nut Cake (below)

French Silk Frosting (below)

*12 whole filberts**

*1 cup finely chopped filberts**

Bake White Nut Cake as directed. Reserve ½ cup French Silk Frosting for decorating; fill layers and frost cake with remaining frosting. Mark servings on frosting with serrated knife.

Place reserved frosting in decorating bag with star tip #18. Pipe three-petaled lily onto each serving. Place 1 whole filbert on each lily. Press chopped filberts into frosting around side. *12 servings.*

WHITE NUT CAKE

6 egg whites

¼ cup sugar

2⅔ cups all-purpose flour

*1½ cups finely chopped filberts**

1¼ cups sugar

½ cup (1 stick) margarine or butter, softened

½ cup shortening

4 teaspoons baking powder

1 teaspoon salt

1 cup milk

Heat oven to 350°. Grease and flour 3 round pans, 8 × 1½ inches. Beat egg whites in large bowl until foamy. Beat in ¼ cup sugar, 1 tablespoon at a time; continue beating until stiff and glossy. Do not underbeat.

Beat flour, filberts, 1¼ cups sugar, the margarine, shortening, baking powder and salt in another large bowl on medium speed 30 seconds, scraping bowl constantly. Beat in milk on medium speed 2 minutes, scraping bowl occasionally; fold into egg whites. Pour batter into pans.

Bake 35 to 40 minutes or until toothpick inserted in center comes out clean. (Refrigerate 1 layer while 2 are baking.) Cool 10 minutes; remove from pans. Cool completely.

FRENCH SILK FROSTING

4 cups powdered sugar

1 cup (2 sticks) margarine or butter, softened

3 tablespoons milk

1½ teaspoons vanilla

3 ounces unsweetened chocolate, melted and cooled

Beat all ingredients on medium speed until frosting is smooth and of spreading consistency. If necessary, stir in additional milk, 1 teaspoon at a time.

___

TIME-SAVER TIP: Substitute 1 package (18.25 ounces) white cake mix with pudding for the White Nut Cake. Prepare and bake as directed on package for two 8-inch rounds—except stir ½ cup finely chopped filberts into batter.

*Finely chopped pecans can be substituted for the finely chopped filberts in the cake batter and around the frosted cake. Substitute pecan halves for the whole filberts on top of the frosted cake.

Caramel-Pecan Torte

Caramel Cake (below)

Caramel Frosting (below)

1 to 2 teaspoons milk

Chopped pecans or chocolate-covered pecan halves

Bake Caramel Cake as directed. Cut cake horizontally into 3 layers. Reserve ½ cup Caramel Frosting. Fill layers with remaining frosting. Stir milk into reserved frosting until of drizzling consistency; drizzle over cake. Garnish with chopped pecans. *18 servings.*

CARAMEL CAKE

2¼ cups all-purpose flour

1¾ cups packed brown sugar

½ cup shortening

1 cup milk

3 teaspoons baking powder

½ teaspoon salt

1 teaspoon vanilla

2 eggs

½ cup chopped pecans

Heat oven to 350°. Grease and flour 12-cup bundt cake pan. Beat all ingredients except pecans in large bowl on low speed 30 seconds, scraping bowl constantly. Beat on high speed 3 minutes, scraping bowl frequently. Stir in pecans. Pour batter into pan.

Bake 35 to 40 minutes or until toothpick inserted in center comes out clean. Cool 20 minutes; invert onto wire rack. Cool completely.

CARAMEL FROSTING

½ cup (1 stick) margarine or butter

1 cup packed brown sugar

¼ cup milk

2 cups powdered sugar

Heat margarine over medium heat in 2-quart saucepan until melted. Stir in brown sugar. Heat to boiling, stirring constantly. Reduce heat to low. Boil and stir 2 minutes. Stir in milk. Heat to boiling; remove from heat. Cool to lukewarm. Gradually stir in powdered sugar. Place saucepan of frosting in bowl of cold water. Beat until smooth and of spreading consistency. If frosting becomes too stiff, stir in additional milk, 1 teaspoon at a time.

CHOCOLATE-DIPPED NUTS OR FRUITS

Melt 1½ ounces bittersweet chocolate, chopped and 2 teaspoons shortening. Coat 12 whole nuts or pieces of dried fruit ¾ of the way; place on waxed-paper lined cookie sheet. Refrigerate uncovered until chocolate is firm, at least 30 minutes but no longer than 24 hours. See pages 143 and 144 for chocolate tips.

Caramel-Pecan Torte and Chocolate Cookie Cake (page 116)

Chocolate Cookie Cake

When you need a smaller cake, just cut the recipe in half and bake it in one layer.

Cookie–Sour Cream Cake (below)

¾ cup whipping (heavy) cream

1 tablespoon sugar

3 creme-filled sandwich cookies, cut in half

Bake Cookie–Sour Cream Cake as directed. Beat whipping cream and sugar in chilled bowl until stiff. Place 1 cake layer on serving plate; spread with half of the whipped cream. Repeat with remaining layer and whipped cream. Garnish with cookie halves and, if desired, cookie crumbs. *16 servings.*

COOKIE–SOUR CREAM CAKE

2 cups all-purpose flour

1½ cups sugar

1 cup sour cream

½ cup (1 stick) margarine or butter, softened

½ cup water

1 teaspoon baking soda

1 teaspoon baking powder

2 eggs

16 creme-filled sandwich cookies

Heat oven to 350°. Grease and flour 2 round pans, 8 × 1½ or 9 × 1½ inches. Beat all ingredients except cookies in large bowl on low speed 30 seconds, scraping bowl constantly. Beat on high speed 2 minutes, scraping bowl occasionally. Coarsely chop cookies. Stir into batter. Pour into pans.

Bake 30 to 35 minutes or until cake springs back when touched lightly in center. Cool 10 minutes; remove from pans. Cool completely.

Decadent Chocolate Cake with Raspberry Sauce and Maple-Pecan Cake (page 118)

Decadent Chocolate Cake with Raspberry Sauce

If you know that you will be serving the whole cake at once, pipe 12 whipped cream rosettes around the cake, one on each serving, and pile a few raspberries in the center just before serving. It'll be a showstopper!

1 cup semisweet chocolate chips

½ cup (1 stick) margarine or butter

½ cup all-purpose flour or cake flour

4 eggs, separated

½ cup sugar

½ cup semisweet chocolate chips

2 tablespoons margarine or butter

2 tablespoons light corn syrup

Raspberry Sauce (below)

½ cup whipped cream

Heat oven to 325°. Grease springform pan, 8 × 2½ inches, or round pan, 9 × 1½ inches. Heat 1 cup chocolate chips and ½ cup margarine in 2-quart heavy saucepan over medium heat until chocolate chips are melted; cool 5 minutes. Stir in flour until smooth. Stir in egg yolks until well blended.

Beat egg whites in large bowl on high speed until foamy. Beat in sugar, 1 tablespoon at a time, until soft peaks form. Fold chocolate mixture into egg whites. Spread batter in pan.

Bake springform 35 to 40 minutes, round 30 to 35 minutes (top will appear dry and cracked) or until toothpick inserted in center comes out clean; cool 10 minutes. Run knife along side of cake to loosen; remove side of springform pan. Invert cake onto wire rack; remove bottom of springform pan. Cool completely. Place on serving plate.

Heat ½ cup chocolate chips, 2 tablespoons margarine and the corn syrup over medium heat until chocolate chips are melted. Spread over top of cake, allowing some to drizzle down side. Place whipped cream in decorating bag. Pipe a rosette on each serving; spinkle with cocoa if desired. Serve with Raspberry Sauce. Garnish with fresh raspberries if desired. *12 servings.*

RASPBERRY SAUCE

1 package (10 ounces) frozen raspberries, thawed, drained and juice reserved

¼ cup sugar

2 tablespoons cornstarch

1 to 2 tablespoons orange- or raspberry-flavored liqueur, if desired

Add enough water to reserved juice to measure 1 cup. Mix sugar and cornstarch in 1-quart saucepan. Stir in juice and raspberries. Heat to boiling over medium heat. Boil and stir 1 minute; strain. Stir in liqueur.

Maple-Pecan Cake

Maple-Buttermilk Cake (below)
Maple-Butter Frosting (right)
1 cup finely chopped pecans
Chocolate Twigs (page 144), if desired
Malted-milk balls, if desired

Bake Maple-Buttermilk Cake as directed. Fill layers and frost side only with Maple-Butter Frosting. Place pecans on waxed paper. Hold cake as shown in diagram; roll side carefully in pecans to coat. Frost top of cake with remaining frosting in spiral design using large spatula. Garnish with Chocolate Twigs and malted-milk balls. *14 to 16 servings.*

MAPLE-BUTTERMILK CAKE

2½ cups all-purpose flour or 2¾ cups cake flour

1½ cups sugar

½ cup (1 stick) margarine or butter, softened

¼ cup shortening

1½ cups buttermilk

1½ teaspoons baking soda

¾ teaspoon salt

1½ teaspoons maple flavoring

3 eggs

Heat oven to 350°. Grease and flour 2 round pans, 9 × 1½ inches, or 3 round pans, 8 × 1½ inches. Beat all ingredients in large bowl on medium speed 30 seconds, scraping bowl constantly. Beat on high speed 3 minutes, scraping bowl occasionally. Pour batter into pans.

Bake 30 to 35 minutes or until toothpick inserted in center comes out clean. Cool 10 minutes; remove from pans. Cool completely.

MAPLE BUTTER FROSTING

3 cups powdered sugar
⅓ cup margarine or butter, softened
⅓ cup maple-flavored syrup

Mix all ingredients. Beat until frosting is smooth and of spreading consistency. If necessary, stir in additional syrup, ½ teaspoon at a time.

COATING SIDES OF CAKES

Two filled cake layers can be rolled in chopped nuts, candies or flaked coconut to coat sides. Place nuts on waxed paper. Hold cake as shown in illustration. Roll side carefully in nuts to coat. (See photo of Maple-Pecan Cake on page 116.)

Strawberries and Cream Cake

Do you love raspberries or peaches? Any berries or cut-up fruit can be substituted for the strawberries in this luscious cake.

Whipped Cream Cake (below)
Whipped Cream Cheese Frosting (right)
1 pint strawberries, sliced

Bake Whipped Cream Cake as directed. Spread 1 layer with ½ cup of the Whipped Cream Cheese Frosting; top with layer of sliced strawberries. Place remaining cake layer on top. Spread thin layer of frosting on side of cake.

Place remaining frosting in decorating bag with large open star tip #4B. Pipe vertical rows on side of cake. Pipe shell border around top edge of cake. Arrange sliced strawberries on top of cake. Refrigerate remaining cake. *16 servings.*

WHIPPED CREAM CAKE

> *2 cups all-purpose flour or 2¼ cups cake flour*
>
> *1½ cups sugar*
>
> *2 teaspoons baking powder*
>
> *½ teaspoon salt*
>
> *1½ cups whipping (heavy) cream*
>
> *3 eggs*
>
> *1½ teaspoons vanilla*

Heat oven to 350°. Grease and flour 2 round pans, 8 × 1½ or 9 × 1½ inches. Mix flour, sugar, baking powder and salt. Beat whipping cream in chilled large bowl until stiff. Beat eggs in small bowl about 5 minutes or until very thick and lemon colored. Fold eggs and vanilla into whipped cream. Add flour mixture, about ½ cup at a time, folding gently after each addition until blended. Pour batter into pans.

Bake 30 to 35 minutes or until toothpick inserted in center comes out clean. Cool 10 minutes; remove from pans. Cool completely.

WHIPPED CREAM CHEESE FROSTING

> *1 package (3 ounces) cream cheese, softened*
>
> *1 tablespoon milk*
>
> *2 cups whipping (heavy) cream*
>
> *⅔ cup powdered sugar*

Beat cream cheese and milk in chilled bowl on low speed until smooth; beat in whipping cream and powdered sugar. Beat on high speed, scraping bowl occasionally, until stiff peaks form.

TIME-SAVER TIP: Substitute 1 package (18.25 ounces) yellow cake mix with pudding for the Whipped Cream Cake. Prepare and bake as directed on package.

Lemon Meringue Cake

Meringue Cake (below)

1 package (4-serving size) lemon pudding and pie filling (not instant)

½ cup whipped cream

Bake Meringue Cake as directed. Prepare pudding and pie filling as directed on package. Refrigerate about 1½ hours or until chilled. Stir pudding; spread 1¼ cups over meringue on 1 cake layer. Place remaining layer, meringue side up, on pudding. Spread with remaining pudding. Place whipped cream in decorating bag with star tip. Pipe on whipped cream, or garnish with whipped cream as desired. Serve within 30 minutes. *8 to 10 servings.*

MERINGUE CAKE

1½ cups cake flour

¾ cup sugar

1½ teaspoons baking powder

½ teaspoon salt

¾ cup shortening

⅔ cup milk

1½ teaspoons vanilla

4 eggs, separated

1 cup sugar

Heat oven to 325°. Grease sides of 2 round pans, 9 × 1½ or 8 × 1½ inches. Line bottoms of pans with cooking parchment paper or waxed paper circles. Beat flour, ¾ cup sugar, the baking powder, salt, shortening, milk, vanilla and egg yolks in medium bowl on low speed 30 seconds, scraping bowl constantly. Beat on high speed 2 minutes, scraping bowl occasionally (batter will be stiff). Spread evenly in pans.

Beat egg whites in small bowl on medium speed until foamy. Beat in 1 cup sugar, 1 tablespoon at a time, on high speed until stiff peaks form. Spread half of the egg white mixture over batter in each pan.

Bake 30 to 35 minutes or until meringue looks set and dry. Cool 10 minutes. Loosen meringues from edges of pans with knife point if necessary. Carefully remove from pans and peel off paper. Place layers, meringue sides up, on wire racks. Cool completely.

Lemon Meringue Cake and Strawberries and Cream Cake (page 119)

FRESH FRUIT DECORATIONS

A great variety of fresh fruits are now available. Choose fruits at their seasonal peak for the fullest flavors and the most economical prices. Choose ripe, but firm, fruits that will hold their shapes.

Whole raspberries, blueberries or blackberries, whole and sliced strawberries, sliced kiwifruit, starfruit or papaya and orange segments are good choices because they do not turn brown. If using sliced peaches, nectarines, apples, bananas or mangos, dip fruit in water mixed with lemon juice; drain well.

Place fruits on cake just before serving. Refrigerate any remaining cake.

Mocha Cream Torte

Golden Pound Cake (page 126)
Mocha Cream Frosting (below)
Chocolate Curls (page 144)
Chocolate coffee beans

Prepare Golden Pound Cake as directed—except grease and flour loaf pan, 9 × 5 × 3 inches, omit almond extract and increase bake time to 60 to 65 minutes. Freeze cooled cake uncovered about 1½ hours or until firm. Cut cake horizontally into 5 layers. Spread scant ¼ cup Mocha Cream Frosting between each layer; frost sides and top of cake with remaining frosting.

Mark diagonal lines with tines of fork across top and down sides of cake. Garnish with Chocolate Curls made with white chocolate and chocolate coffee beans. *16 servings.*

MOCHA CREAM FROSTING

1 tablespoon instant coffee
2 tablespoons hot water
4 cups powdered sugar
¾ cup margarine or butter, softened
1 tablespoon cocoa
1 teaspoon water

Dissolve instant coffee in the hot water. Beat coffee and remaining ingredients on medium speed until smooth and of spreading consistency. If necessary, stir in additional water, ½ teaspoon at a time.

TIME-SAVER TIP: Substitute 1 package (16 ounces) golden pound cake mix for the Golden Pound Cake. Prepare and bake as directed on package.

Walnut Torte

1½ cups chopped walnuts
1½ cups vanilla wafer crumbs
1 cup packed brown sugar
1 cup (2 sticks) margarine or butter, melted
Dark Cocoa Cake (page 147)
1½ cups whipping (heavy) cream
3 tablespoons granulated sugar
1 teaspoon vanilla

Heat oven to 350°. Line 2 ungreased round pans, 9 × 1½ inches, with kitchen parchment or waxed paper. Mix walnuts, wafer crumbs, brown sugar and margarine. Spread about ¾ cup mixture in each pan; reserve remaining walnut mixture. Prepare Dark Cocoa Cake as directed. Pour about 1¼ cups batter over walnut mixture in each pan; refrigerate remaining batter.

Bake about 20 minutes or until top springs back when touched lightly. Immediately remove from pans; invert. Repeat with remaining walnut mixture and batter. Cool layers completely.

Beat whipping cream, granulated sugar and vanilla in chilled small bowl until stiff. Place 1 cake layer, walnut side up, on serving plate; spread with about ¾ cup whipped cream. Repeat with remaining layers and whipped cream. Or, place whipped cream for top layer in decorating bag with star tip #6. Pipe rosettes in center of cake and garnish with Chocolate Leaves (page 78) if desired. Refrigerate until chilled. *16 servings.*

TIME-SAVER TIP: Substitute 1 package (18.25 ounces) devil's food cake mix with pudding for the Dark Cocoa Cake. Prepare batter as directed on package. Continue as directed above.

Mocha Cream Torte and Walnut Torte

Glazed Whole Wheat Fruitcake

1½ cups whole wheat flour

1½ cups all-purpose flour

1¼ cups sugar

¾ cup margarine or butter, softened

¾ cup shortening

⅔ cup orange juice

1½ teaspoons baking powder

¾ teaspoon salt

9 eggs

16 ounces candied cherries, cut into halves (about 2½ cups)

15 ounces golden raisins (about 3 cups)

12 ounces candied pineapple, cut up (about 2 cups)

4 ounces candied citron, cut up (about ⅔ cup)

4 ounces candied orange peel, cut up (about ⅔ cup)

¾ cup flaked coconut

8 ounces blanched whole almonds (about 1½ cups)

8 ounces pecan halves (about 2 cups)

¼ cup apple jelly, melted

Heat oven to 275°. Line 2 loaf pans, 9 × 5 × 3 inches, with aluminum foil; grease. Beat flours, sugar, margarine, shortening, orange juice, baking powder, salt and eggs in large bowl on medium speed, scraping bowl constantly, until blended, about 30 seconds. Beat on high speed, scraping bowl occasionally, 3 minutes. Mix batter into fruits and nuts in 6-quart bowl. Spread mixture in pans.

Bake 2½ to 3 hours or until wooden pick inserted in center comes out clean. Remove from pans; cool.

Spread with melted apple jelly and decorate with blanched almonds or candied fruit, if desired. *2 loaves.*

Fruitcake Ring

Mincemeat Fruitcake (below)
Browned Butter Glaze (below)
⅓ cup coarsely chopped pecans

Bake Mincemeat Fruitcake as directed. Spread with Browned Butter Glaze, letting it run down side unevenly. Immediately sprinkle top with pecans.

MINCEMEAT FRUITCAKE

2 eggs

1 jar (28 ounces) ready-to-use mincemeat

16 ounces mixed candied fruit (about 2 cups)

1 can (14 ounces) sweetened condensed milk

1 cup coarsely chopped pecans

2½ cups all-purpose flour

1 teaspoon baking soda

Heat oven to 300°. Generously grease and flour 12-cup bundt cake pan or tube pan, 10 × 4 inches. Beat eggs slightly in large bowl. Stir in mincemeat, candied fruit, sweetened condensed milk and pecans. Stir in flour and baking soda. Pour batter into pan.

Bake about 1 hour 50 minutes or until wooden pick inserted in center comes out clean. Cool 15 minutes; remove from pan. Cool completely.

BROWNED BUTTER GLAZE

2 tablespoons margarine or butter
1 cup powdered sugar
1 teaspoon vanilla
1 tablespoon hot water

Heat margarine in saucepan over medium heat until delicate brown. Cool slightly. Stir in powdered sugar, vanilla and water. If necessary, stir in additional hot water, 1 teaspoon at a time, until glaze is desired consistency.

Glazed Whole Wheat Fruitcake and Fruitcake Ring

Marzipan Torte

Golden Pound Cake (right)
1 jar (12 ounces) apricot preserves
1 package (7 ounces) marzipan
½ cup sliced almonds
½ cup powdered sugar
2 teaspoons water
2 teaspoons cocoa
Red food color

Bake Golden Pound Cake as directed. Split cake horizontally to make 4 layers (see page 132). If necessary, break up any large pieces of apricot in preserves. Fill each layer with scant ¼ cup of the apricot preserves. Brush side and top of cake lightly with preserves.

Reserve half of the marzipan for top of cake. Shape half of the remaining marzipan into rectangle, about 4 × 1 inch. Roll between sheets of waxed paper into rectangle, 12 × 3 inches (marzipan will be very thin). Trim sides to make even, pressing trimmings on ends if necessary to make 12 × 3-inch rectangle.

Peel top sheet of waxed paper off marzipan. Using bottom sheet of waxed paper to help transfer, lift marzipan and waxed paper together as shown in diagram and carefully press marzipan onto half of cake side (press any excess over top edge of cake). Remove waxed paper. Repeat with remaining fourth of marzipan. Smooth edges together with spatula to join.

Add any remaining marzipan trimmings to reserved half of marzipan; shape into flattened round. Roll between sheets of waxed paper into 8-inch circle. Peel top sheet of waxed paper off marzipan. Lift remaining waxed paper and marzipan together, invert and press onto top of cake. Press to join marzipan around top edge of cake. Carefully remove waxed paper. Brush side only of cake lightly with apricot preserves; press almonds into marzipan to coat side of cake.

Mix powdered sugar and water; reserve 1 tablespoon for flowers. Stir cocoa and enough additional water, a few drops at a time, into remaining frosting until of spreading consistency. Place in small, sturdy plastic storage bag; cut off very small corner of bag to make writing tip. Draw desired design lightly in marzipan with toothpick. Fold over top of bag; press out frosting to follow design.

Stir 3 or 4 drops red food color into reserved frosting. Place in another small, sturdy plastic storage bag; cut off very small corner of bag to make writing tip. Pipe 3 to 5 dots to form each flower. *16 servings.*

Note: Keep marzipan covered at all times to prevent it from drying out. If marzipan sticks to hands, sprinkle hands lightly with powdered sugar. Marzipan can be rerolled easily if necessary. When rolling marzipan for side of cake, lift rolling pin slightly at ends of marzipan to prevent ends from becoming too thin. When rolling marzipan for top, roll from center to outside evenly in all directions.

GOLDEN POUND CAKE

2 cups all-purpose flour
1 cup sugar
¼ cup (½ stick) margarine of butter, softened
¼ cup shortening
¾ cup milk
3 teaspoons baking powder
1 teaspoon salt
1 teaspoon almond extract
1 teaspoon vanilla
2 eggs

Heat oven to 350°. Grease and flour 2 round pans, 8 × 1½ inches. Beat all ingredients in large bowl on medium speed 30 seconds, scraping bowl constantly. Beat on high speed 3 minuttes, scraping bowl occasionally. Pour batter into pans.

Bake 30 to 35 minutes or until toothpick inserted in center comes out clean. Cool 10 minutes; remove from pans. Cool completely.

TIME-SAVER TIP; Substitute 1 package (16 ounces) golden pound cake mix for the Golden Pound Cake. Prepare as directed on package— except add 1 teaspoon almond extract before beating. Bake in 2 round pans, 8 × 1½ inches, 30 to 35 minutes.

PLACING MARZIPAN ON MARZIPAN CAKE

Lift marzipan and waxed paper together; press marzipan onto half of cake side. Remove wax paper. Repeat with remaining side.

Marzipan Torte and Chocolate Mint Loaves (page 128)

Chocolate Mint Loaves

Use holiday mints for different seasons of the year. Try orange for Halloween, for instance.

Peppermint Chiffon Cake (below)
Chocolate-Mint Frosting (right)
7 to 10 squares chocolate party mints

Bake Peppermint Chiffon Cake as directed. Remove loaves from pans. Reserve 3 cups Chocolate-mint Frosting for decorating; frost loaves with remaining frosting. Place reserved frosting in decorating bag with large open star tip #4B. Pipe frosting in continuous motion back and forth across tops of loaves. Cut party mints diagonally in half if desired; decorate tops of loaves. Refrigerate any remaining cake. *16 servings.*

PEPPERMINT CHIFFON CAKE

> *2 cup all-purpose flour*
> *1½ cups sugar*
> *3 teaspoons baking powder*
> *1 teaspoon salt*
> *¾ cup cold water*
> *½ cup vegetable oil*
> *½ teaspoon peppermint extract*
> *7 egg yolks*
> *1 cup egg whites (about 8)*
> *½ teaspoon cream of tartar*

Heat oven to 325°. Mix flour, sugar, baking powder and salt in large bowl. Beat in water, oil, peppermint extract and egg yolk with spoon until smooth.

Beat egg whites and cream of tartar in another large bowl on medium speed until stiff peaks form. Pour egg yolk mixture gradually over beaten egg whites, folding with rubber spatula just until blended. Divide batter between 2 ungreased loaf pans, 9 × 5 × 3 inches.

Bake 50 to 55 minutes or until top springs back when touched lightly. Invert pans with edges on 2 other pans; let hang until cakes are cold.

CHOCOLATE-MINT FROSTING

> *3 cups whipping (heavy) cream*
> *1½ cups powdered sugar*
> *¾ cup cocoa*
> *½ teaspoons peppermint extract*

Beat all ingredients in chilled bowl until stiff.

5

Cake Basics

The Basics

The equipment, tips and techniques described here are your guide to the best and easiest ways to bake, frost and decorate your beautiful special occasion cakes. Practice will give you confidence and assure you of terrific results every time.

You can also mix cakes by hand. Stir the ingredients to moisten and blend them; then beat 150 strokes for every minute of beating time (3 minutes equals 450 strokes). You'll need practice before this seems easy; while you're practicing, cake volume may not be as high.

MEASURING INGREDIENTS

Use graduated nested measuring cups for measuring nonliquids. For all-purpose flour and granulated sugar, dip the cup into the ingredient to fill, then level. (Do not sift flour to measure or to combine with other ingredients.)

For cake flour and powdered sugar, lightly spoon into the cup, then level. (Sift powdered sugar only if it is lumpy—if it is sifted the quantity may need to be increased.)

Graduated spoons are used to measure thin liquids. Pour the liquid into the appropriate spoon until full.

For dry ingredients and thick liquids, pour or scoop into the appropriate spoon until full, then level with a straight-edged knife or spatula. If your set of spoons does not have a ⅛ teaspoon measure, use the ¼ teaspoon, fill it and remove half.

Glass measuring cups are used for measuring liquids. Read the measurement at eye level.

Spoon brown sugar and shortening into the cup, then pack down firmly. For nuts, coconut and cut-up or small fruit, lightly spoon into the cup, then pack down lightly.

BEATING CAKE BATTER

Surveys show that the majority of mixers in use in the United States are the portable type; our cakes have been tested with both the portable and standard electric mixer. Standard mixers are usually more powerful than portable. So, for the initial step of beating layer cake ingredients

EGG VOLUMES	
Number of Large eggs	**Liquid Cup Measurement**
2 eggs	⅓ to ½ cup
3 eggs	½ to ⅔ cup
4 eggs	⅔ to 1 cup
1 egg white	about 2 tablespoons
1 egg yolk	about 1½ tablespoons

until blended, reduce the speed of the standard mixer to low to prevent splattering.

You can also mix cakes by hand. Stir the ingredients to moisten and blend them; then beat 150 strokes for every minute of beating time (3 minutes equals 450 strokes). You'll need practice before this seems easy; while you're practicing, cake volume may not be as high.

USING EGGS
Our cake recipes have been tested with large eggs. Eggs are also available in medium and extra large. If using a size other than large, use the following chart for the correct equivalent.

For better volume, let egg whites stand at room temperature about 15 minutes before beating. Beat whites in a clean, dry metal bowl with a clean beater. Any yolk or fat in the whites will prevent them from beating properly.

Leftover egg whites can be stored covered in the refrigerator 7 to 10 days. Leftover egg yolks should be covered with water and can be stored in a covered container in the refrigerator 2 to 3 days. To freeze whites, place in a plastic ice cube tray, then remove the frozen cubes to a plastic freezer bag for storage. Thaw frozen whites in the refrigerator.

Leftover yolks can be used in custards, scrambled eggs, boiled dressings, egg pastries and cake fillings.

USING SHORTENINGS
When our recipes call for margarine or butter, they have been tested using stick-type marga-rine and butter. When they call for shortening, they have been tested with solid vegetable shortening. Unless oil is called for (as with chiffon-type cakes) never substitute oil for shortening, margarine or butter, even if the recipe calls for melted shortening.

BAKING CAKES
Always use the size pans called for in the recipe. To check the width of a pan, measure across the top from inside edge to inside edge. Baking a cake in too large a pan will result in a pale, flat, shrunken cake. Too small or too shallow a pan will result in a cake that bulges and loses its shape.

Shiny metal pans reflect heat away from the cake. They produce a tender, light brown crust and are preferred for baking cakes.

Dark nonstick or glass baking pans should be used by following the manufacturers' directions. These pans readily absorb heat and a better result is often achieved if the baking temperature is reduced 25°.

Fill cake pans no more than half full. If you are using a pan with an unusual shape (heart, star, bell), measure the capacity by filling with water, measure the water and use half that amount in batter. (Cupcakes can be made from any remaining batter.)

For shortening-type cakes, such as yellow and white cakes, oven racks should be in the middle of the oven and pans placed in the center of the rack. Layer pans should not touch and there should be at least 1 inch of space between the pans and the oven sides.

REMOVING LAYER CAKES FROM PANS

Cool the cake layers in pans on wire racks 10 minutes. Cover one rack with a towel; place towel side down on top of layer; invert as a unit. Remove pan.

Place a rack on bottom of layer; turn over both racks so the layer is right side up. Repeat with other layer(s). Allow layers to cool completely on racks.

SPLITTING LAYER CAKES

Wooden pick markers: Mark middle points on sides of layer with wooden picks. Using picks as a guide, cut through the layer with long, thin sharp knife.

Thread trick: Split the layer by pulling a piece of heavy sewing thread horizontally, back and forth, through the layer.

FROSTING LAYER CAKES

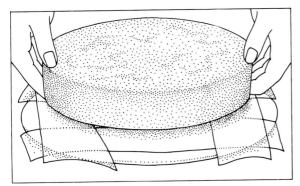

Place 4 strips of waxed paper around the edge of cake plate. Brush away any loose crumbs from the cooled cake layer. Place the layer on a plate, rounded side down. (The waxed paper will protect the plate as you frost and can be removed later.)

Spread about ⅓ cup creamy frosting (½ cup if fluffy frosting) over the top of the first layer to within about ¼ inch of the edge.

Place the second layer, rounded side up, on the first layer so that the 2 flat sides of the layers are together with frosting in between. Coat the side of the cake with a very thin layer of frosting to seal in the crumbs.

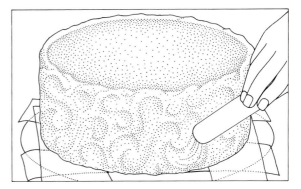

Frost the side of the cake in swirls, making a rim about ¼ inch high above the top of the cake to prevent the top from appearing sloped. Spread the remaining frosting on top, just to the built-up rim.

COOLING AND REMOVING ANGEL FOOD AND CHIFFON CAKES FROM PAN

Invert the pan on a heatproof funnel or bottle and let hang until cake is cold.

Loosen the cake by moving a spatula or table knife up and down against side of pan.

SPLITTING ANGEL FOOD AND CHIFFON CAKES INTO LAYERS

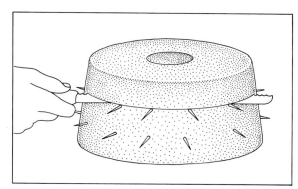

Measure the cake with a ruler and mark into 3 equal widths with wooden picks. Using a serrated knife and with wooden picks as a guide,

cut across the cake with a light, sawing motion. The same technique can be used for splitting into 4 layers.

USE OF DOWELS

If you wish, dowels or legs can be added to large tiered cakes for support and stability. Dowels should be about ⅛ inch higher than each tier (see illustration). Insert the dowel through tier to plate or cardboard round. Use 4 to 8 dowels per tier, depending on the size of the layer.

Arrange the dowels in a circle, square or rectangle slightly smaller than the tier placed directly on top of them. Place the next tier on cardboard round on top of dowels. Repeat with remaining tiers except the top tier. Dowels can be of wood or plastic. If using separators or columns, refer to the manufacturer's directions.

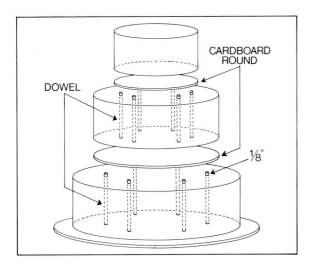

CUTTING AND FROSTING CUT-UP CAKES

Cakes may be frozen before cutting to minimize crumbling during cutting. Freeze cut pieces on a cookie sheet for about an hour before frosting. Exposed cut edges may be crumb coated before frosting to help control crumbling. To do this, mix water, a teaspoon at a time, into a small amount of frosting, to make a thin frosting. Spread a smooth, thin layer onto cut surfaces; freeze.

Keep frostings covered with plastic wrap while working to prevent them from crusting and becoming dry.

FREEZING UNFROSTED AND FROSTED CAKES

Unfrosted cakes and cupcakes freeze better than frosted cakes. Allow the cakes to cool completely. Place cakes in rigid containers (such as cardboard bakery boxes) to prevent crushing, then cover with aluminum foil, plastic wrap or large freezer bags. Properly packaged, unfrosted cakes can be kept frozen 3 to 4 months. Cakes can also be frozen in family portions or single pieces that thaw out quickly.

Of the frosted cakes, those with creamy-type frostings freeze best. Fluffy-type and whipped cream frostings freeze well but tend to stick to the wrappings. To prevent frosting from sticking to the wrapping, freeze cake uncovered 1 hour, insert wooden picks around the top and side of cake, and wrap. Frozen frosted cakes keep for 2 to 3 months.

Decorating gel, hard candies and colored sugars do not freeze well. They tend to run during thawing.

STORING UNFROSTED AND FROSTED CAKES

Cool unfrosted cakes completely before storing. If covered when warm, they become sticky. To store cakes that will be frosted later, cover them loosely so the surface stays dry. Otherwise, they become sticky and difficult to frost.

Store cakes with a creamy-type frosting under a cake safe (or large inverted bowl) or cover loosely with aluminum foil, plastic wrap or waxed paper.

Cakes with whipped cream toppings or cream fillings should be stored in the refrigerator.

Fluffy frostings are not as stable as creamy frostings because so much air is incorporated into them. It is best to frost a cake with fluffy frosting on the day it is to be served. However, if you must store the cake overnight, place it under a cake safe or inverted bowl and slip a wooden spoon handle or a knife blade under the rim so the cover is not airtight.

CUTTING FROSTED CAKES

Use a sharp, thin knife to cut shortening-type cakes and a long serrated knife for angels and chiffons. If the frosting sticks, dip the knife into hot water and wipe with a damp paper towel after cutting each slice. Cover exposed cut ends with plastic wrap to maintain moistness.

BACKGROUNDS FOR CUT-UP CAKES

Cakes may be served on trays, large bread-boards or inverted jelly-roll pans. If you do not have a tray large enough, use a piece of card-board cut 2 to 4 inches larger than the assembled cake. Cover the background with aluminum or colored foil, colored plastic wrap or freezer paper. To vary the color or fit the occasion, use other paper, such as shelf paper, gift wrap, col-ored tissue paper or a home-drawn creation, and then cover with clear cellophane or plastic wrap. If you wish, messages or other designs can be added to the background around the cake with either a marking pencil or piped frosting.

DECORATING BASICS

1. It is important that the frosting to be used for decorating is the right consistency. Borders and drop flowers can have a medium consis-tency frosting, roses and other flowers need a firmer frosting so the petals will hold their shape and frosting to be used for writing, leaves and simple line designs can be slightly thinner.

2. Powdered sugar must be completely free of lumps when it is to be used for a decorating frosting. If there are even small lumps it will be necessary to sift it.

3. Most designs are made by holding the decorating bag at a 45° angle as shown above. For drop flowers, stars, dots and rosettes, hold the bag at a 90° angle (perpendicular to the surface).

CAKE YIELDS	
Size and Type of Cake	**Number of Servings**
8-inch layer	10 to 14
9-inch layer	12 to 16
9-inch loaf	8 to 10
8- or 9-inch square	9
13 × 9-inch rectangular	12 to 15
10-inch tube	12 to 16
12-cup fluted tube	12 to 16

4. Before piping a design or a message on a cake, lightly outline the design with a wooden pick to use as a guide. Short strips of sewing thread can be lightly placed on the frosted cake to mark the position of the message.

5. Use steady pressure to press out the frosting. The amount of pressure will determine the size and evenness of any design. To finish a design, stop the pressure and lift the point up and away.

6. When adding food color, remember that frosting will darken slightly as it sets. For vivid or deeper food colors, use paste food color.

7. A turntable or lazy Susan is a helpful tool to make it easier and faster to frost and decorate cakes.

DECORATING BAGS

Decorating bags used for cake decorating include reusable plastic-coated decorating bags and disposable parchment paper or plastic bags. The plastic-coated decorating bag can be used with or without a coupler. The coupler saves time by enabling you to change decorating tips while still using the same bag of frosting. A coupler is not used for large decorating tips.

If you do not have a decorating bag, you can make a cone from a plastic bag or paper envelope. Place ½ cup frosting in the corner of the bag and seal, or, place ⅓ cup frosting in the corner of an envelope and fold the sides of the envelope toward the center. Snip a small piece off the corner to make a tip.

HOW TO FIT YOUR NEW DECORATING BAG WITH A COUPLER

1. Unscrew the ring off the coupler base and drop the base, narrow end first, down into the end of the bag. Push the coupler base as far down into the bag as possible.

2. With a pencil, mark the location of the coupler's bottom thread on the outside of the bag. Push the coupler up and out of the bag.

3. Cut off the end of the decorating bag at the pencil mark. (Be careful not to cut too much; you can always trim a little more later if necessary.)

4. Replace the coupler base in the bag, pushing it down so the 2 bottom threads of the coupler show through the open end of the bag. Place decorating tip in ring and screw onto coupler base.

HOW TO USE YOUR DECORATING BAG

1. If not using a coupler or if the decorating tip is large, simply place the tip in the bag. If using a coupler, place the desired decorating tip on the coupler base and screw the coupler ring into place over the tip to hold it securely. With tip in place you're ready to fill the bag with frosting.

2. To fill the bag with frosting or whipped cream, fold down the open end of the bag to form a cuff approximately 2 inches wide. Hold the bag beneath the cuff and, using a spatula, fill the bag half full with frosting. (It is important not to fill the bag too full as the extra frosting will back up out of the bag.)

3. To change decorating tips, unscrew the coupler ring, remove the tip, replace it with another tip and screw the ring on again.

4. To close the bag, unfold the cuff and twist the top of the bag, forcing the frosting down into the tip. Continue to twist end of bag as you decorate.

HOW TO MAKE ROSETTES AND DROP FLOWERS

Rosettes: Using a star tip, press out whipped cream or frosting, using steady, even pressure, into a circle. Then, without stopping, spiral the whipped cream on top in a smaller circle, finally ending the swirl in a peak as you decrease the pressure.

Drop Flowers: Using a drop flower tip, hold the decorating bag perpendicular (straight up) with the tip touching surface. Squeeze the bag, keeping the tip in frosting until petals are formed. Stop pressure and pull away.

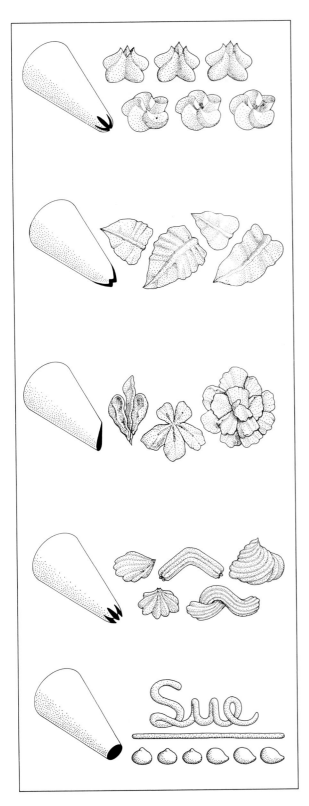

DECORATING TIPS AND THEIR USES

Drop Flower Tips: These tips make the easiest flowers for a beginning cake decorator. They are made directly on the frosted cake. The number of petals is determined by the number of openings in the end of the tip. Drop flower tips can be used to make either plain or swirled drop flowers. Popular drop flower tips include numbers 107, 129, 190, 217, 224, 225, 1C and 2D.

Leaf Tips: The V-shaped opening of this tip forms the pointed end of the leaf. Leaf tips make plain, ruffled or stand-up leaves. Leaf tips can also be used to make attractive borders. Popular leaf tips include 65, 67 and 352.

Petal Tips: These tips are used for making roses, wild roses, violets, sweet peas and carnations. They are also used for making ribbons, bows, swags and ruffles. Popular petal tips include numbers 101, 102, 103 and 104. For very large roses, number 127 can be used.

Star Tips: These tips are used for making shell, rope and zigzag borders, stars and rosettes and can also be used for making drop flowers. Popular star tips include numbers 13 through 22 and can range in size from small to very large. Large star tips include numbers 32, 43 and 8B.

Writing Tips: Writing tips are also called plain or round tips. In addition to writing messages, these tips can be used for making beads, dots, balls, stems, vines and flower centers. Popular writing tips include numbers 1 through 4 (small), 5 through 12 (medium) and 1A and 2A (large).

BORDERS

Shell Border: As the name implies, this is a series of shells connected in a continuous line. Using a star tip, hold decorating bag at a 45° angle to surface. Press out frosting using consistent heavy pressure to create a full base. Raise the tip as shell builds up. Decrease pressure, drawing frosting to a point. Begin the next shell directly over that point.

Reverse Shell Border: This border is similar to the plain Shell Border except that as the shell is built up, circle to the right and decrease pressure. The second shell is circled to the left. Continue, alternating shells from right to left.

Bead Border: This technique is the same as the Shell Border technique except uses a writing tip. Vary pressure to make different size balls.

Zigzag Border: Using a star or writing tip, hold the decorating bag at a 45° angle to surface. Press out frosting with a steady, even pressure, moving bag from side to side slightly to form a zigzag line.

Rope Border: Using a star or large writing tip, hold the decorating bag at a 45° angle to the surface. Touch the tip to the surface and squeeze the bag, moving the tip down, up and around to the right, forming a slight S curve. Stop pressure and pull the tip away. Place the tip under bottom curve of the first S and repeat the procedure. Continue joining S curves to form rope.

Swag Border: Using a star, petal or writing tip, hold the decorating bag at a 45° angle to the surface. As you press out frosting, move the tip down and up, down and up as if writing a continuous letter U. Use steady, even pressure as you repeat the procedure. When completed, discontinue pressure and pull the tip away.

HOW TO MAKE BASIC LEAF AND SIMPLE DESIGNS

Basic Leaf: Using a leaf tip, hold the decorating bag at an angle to the surface. Squeeze and hold tip in place to let the frosting fan out to form base of leaf. Decrease pressure as you slowly pull the tip away and lift slightly to draw the leaf to a point.

Simple Designs: Using a writing tip, hold the decorating bag at a 45° angle. With the tip raised slightly from the surface squeeze the bag, applying pressure evenly, and direct the tip to outline the desired design. To end the design stop squeezing, touch tip to surface and pull away.

HOW TO USE A FLOWER NAIL

The flower nail is used to make flowers such as roses and marigolds. The frosting used to make flowers on a flower nail should be quite stiff.

To use a flower nail, attach a 2-inch square of waxed paper to the nail with a small dab of frosting. Hold the stem of the nail between the left thumb and forefinger and slowly rotate the nail to the left (counterclockwise). Hold the decorating bag in the right hand and press out frosting to form the petals. (Left-handed decorators should reverse these directions.)

Flowers can be made in advance and air dried or they can be placed directly on the cake.

HOW TO MAKE MARIGOLDS

1. Touch the wide end of petal tip to center of flower nail, lifting narrow end slightly. Pipe a circle of narrow petals, each about ½ inch long, using a continuous back and forth motion. Turn the nail slowly as you pipe.

2. Pipe 2 or 3 more rows of petals, one on top of the other, making the petals in each row shorter than the last.

HOW TO MAKE ROSES

1. Using a petal tip, hold the bag with narrow end of the tip up. Turn the flower nail counterclockwise and press out frosting in a tiny circle to form center of rose.

2. To form the first petal, make a standing half circle to one side of center.

3. Add 2 more petals, forming a triangle.

4. Add more petals, overlapping, until rose is desired size. Remove the waxed paper with rose from the nail. Place on a level surface and let stand until set. Carefully lift the rose from waxed paper with a spatula and place on the cake. Attach with additional frosting if necessary.

NOTE: For very large roses, use tip #127.

HOW TO MAKE WILD ROSES OR APPLE BLOSSOMS

1. Make a small flat circle of frosting in center of flower nail for base of flower (petals are to be connected securely to this).

2. Using a petal tip, hold the bag with wide end of tip touching center of nail and narrow end almost parallel to nail's surface. As you press out the first petal, turn the nail to the left and move the tip out to the edge of nail and back to center. Stop pressure at center to complete petal and move tip away.

3. Make 4 more petals the same way, always working to the right of the previous petal.

4. Change to a writing tip and hold the bag perpendicular (straight up) to the center of the flower. Press out 2 or 3 small dots at center.

Chocolate Tips

USING CHOCOLATE

Chocolate can be easily melted on the stovetop or in the microwave. Melting must be done carefully, however, as any amount of steam or water will cause the chocolate to harden or "tighten." If chocolate hardens while being melted, it can be returned to a creamy consistency by stirring in about 1 teaspoon shortening for each ounce of chocolate being melted. Chocolate chips can be melted as they are; bars or squares of chocolate should be broken or chopped before melting.

To Melt Chocolate:

- Heat chocolate in a heavy saucepan over low heat, stirring occasionally, until almost melted. Remove from heat and stir until completely melted.
- Place chocolate in a small, heatproof bowl in hot water or top of a double boiler over hot (not boiling) water, stirring occasionally, until melted.
- Microwave ½ to 1 cup chocolate chips uncovered on medium (50%) 3 to 4½ minutes, 1 or 2 squares 3 to 4 minutes, stirring after 2½ minutes. Stir until smooth.

CHOCOLATE POINTERS

"Seizing" is the term used when a very small amount of moisture causes chocolate to become thick, lumpy and grainy during melting. Be sure all utensils are completely dry and that no moisture gets into the chocolate while it melts.

"Bloom" is the term for the dusty looking film that develops on chocolate stored at room temperatures that vary from hot to cold, allowing the cocoa butter to melt and rise to the surface of the chocolate. It does not affect the flavor or quality of the chocolate.

CHOCOLATE STORAGE

To maintain good quality, chocolate must be stored properly. It is important to store it in a cool, dry place between 60° and 78°F. If the temperature is higher than 78° or the humidity is above 50%, chocolate should be kept wrapped in moistureproof wrap. Chocolate can be stored in the refrigerator if tightly wrapped to keep out moisture and odors. Cold chocolate becomes hard and brittle, so remove it from the refrigerator and let stand at room temperature before using.

Cocoa is less sensitive to temperature and humidity that chocolate. It is best to store cocoa in a tightly covered container in a cool, dry place.

SUBSTITUTIONS FOR CHOCOLATE	
1 package (6 ounces) semisweet chocolate chips	1 cup semisweet chocolate chips
1 package (8 ounces) unsweetened chocolate	8 squares (1 ounce each) unsweetened chocolate
1 envelope (1 ounce) premelted chocolate	1 square (1 ounce) unsweetened chocolate
1 square (1 ounce) unsweetened chocolate, melted	3 tablespoons unsweetened cocoa plus 1 tablespoon vegetable oil or shortening
3 squares (1 ounce each) semisweet chocolate	½ cup semisweet chocolate chips

CHOCOLATE CURLS

Place a bar or block of chocolate on waxed paper. Make curls by pressing firmly against the chocolate and pulling a vegetable parer toward you in long, thin strokes. Small curls can be made by using the side of the chocolate bar. Transfer each curl carefully with a wooden pick to a waxed paper–lined cookie sheet or directly onto frosted cake.

The curls will be easier to make if the chocolate is slightly warm. Let the chocolate stand in a warm place for about 15 minutes before slicing. Semisweet chocolate can be used, but curls will be smaller. Thicker bars of chocolate will make larger curls. (See photos of Apricot Wedding Cake on page 87 and Walnut Torte on page 123.)

CHOCOLATE CUT-OUTS

Melt 1 bar (4 ounces) sweet cooking chocolate or 4 squares (1 ounce each) semisweet chocolate. Spread over outside bottom of square pan, 8 × 8 × 2 inches. Refrigerate until firm; bring to room temperature. Use cookie cutters in desired shapes and sizes to make cut-outs. Refrigerate until ready to place on dessert. Make your cut-outs extra special by dipping half of each cut-out in melted white chocolate and refrigerating until set.

CHOCOLATE RIBBONS

Melt 4 ounces white chocolate (white baking bar) or semisweet chocolate. Spread with a metal spatula in a thin layer on a large cookie sheet. Refrigerate about 10 minutes or *just* until chocolate is firm. (Do not refrigerate until hard or chocolate will break. If chocolate gets too hard, let stand at room temperature.)

Scrape strips of chocolate with a knife or metal pastry scraper. Hold the knife flat to the sheet and pull slowly toward you, curling ribbons as you go.

CHOCOLATE TWIGS

Melt 2 ounces white chocolate (white baking bar) or 2 ounces semisweet chocolate and 1 teaspoon shortening. Pour into decorating bag with small writing tip. Squeeze melted chocolate onto waxed paper into twig shapes; sprinkle with white decorator's sugar, if desired. Let dry. Peel twigs from waxed paper; arrange on cake.

SHAVED CHOCOLATE

All types of chocolate can be used to make shaved chocolate. Slide a vegetable peeler across the surface of a bar or block of chocolate, using short, quick strokes. Or, use a vegetable shredder with large holes. Sprinkle on frosted cake.

Angel Food Cake

1½ cups powdered sugar

1 cup cake flour

1½ cups egg whites (about 12)

1½ teaspoons cream of tartar

1 cup granulated sugar

1½ teaspoons vanilla

½ teaspoon almond extract

¼ teaspoon salt

Move oven rack to lowest position. Heat oven to 375°. Mix powdered sugar and flour. Beat egg whites and cream of tartar in large bowl on medium speed until foamy. Beat in granulated sugar on high speed, 2 tablespoons at a time, adding vanilla, almond extract and salt with the last addition of sugar. Continue beating until stiff and glossy. Do not underbeat.

Sprinkle sugar-flour mixture, ¼ cup at a time, over meringue, folding in just until sugar-flour mixture disappears. Push batter into ungreased tube pan, 10 × 4 inches. Cut gently through batter with metal spatula.

Bake 30 to 35 minutes or until cracks in cake feel dry and top springs back when touched lightly. Immediately turn pan upside down onto glass bottle or metal funnel. Let hang about 2 hours or until cake is completely cool. Remove from pan. Spread top of cake with Vanilla Glaze (page 00) if desired.

CHOCOLATE ANGEL FOOD CAKE: Substitute ¼ cup cocoa for ¼ cup of the flour. Omit almond extract.

SPICY ANGEL FOOD CAKE: Add 1 teaspoon pumpkin pie spice with flour. Omit almond extract.

Applesauce Cake

2½ cups all-purpose flour or cake flour

1¼ cups sugar

1½ teaspoons baking soda

1½ teaspoons salt

¾ teaspoon ground cinnamon

½ teaspoon ground cloves

½ teaspoon ground allspice

¼ teaspoon baking powder

1½ cups applesauce

½ cup water

½ cup shortening

2 eggs

1 cup raisins

½ cup chopped walnuts

Heat oven to 350°. Grease and flour desired pan(s). Beat all ingredients in large bowl on low speed 30 seconds, scraping bowl constantly. Beat on high speed 3 minutes, scraping bowl occasionally. Pour batter into pan(s).

Bake as directed below or until toothpick inserted in center comes out clean. Cool 10 minutes; remove from pan(s). Cool completely.

13 × 9 × 2-inch rectangle	60 to 65 minutes
two 8 × 1½-inch rounds	50 to 55 minutes
two 9 × 1½-inch rounds	50 to 55 minutes
9 × 1½-inch round	50 to 55 minutes
6 × 3-inch ovenproof bowl	70 to 80 minutes

WHOLE WHEAT APPLESAUCE CAKE: Substitute 1¼ cups whole wheat flour for 1¼ cups of the all-purpose flour. Do not use cake flour.

Buttermilk Spice Cake

2½ cups all-purpose flour or cake flour

1 cup granulated sugar

¾ cup packed brown sugar

½ cup shortening

1⅓ cups buttermilk

1 teaspoon baking powder

1 teaspoon baking soda

1 teaspoon salt

¾ teaspoon ground cinnamon

¾ teaspoon ground allspice

½ teaspoon ground cloves

½ teaspoon ground nutmeg

3 eggs

Heat oven to 350°. Grease and flour desired pan(s). Beat all ingredients in large bowl on medium speed 30 seconds, scraping bowl constantly. Beat on high speed 3 minutes, scraping bowl occasionally. Pour batter into pan(s).

Bake as directed below or until toothpick inserted in center comes out clean. Cool 10 minutes; remove from pan(s). Cool completely.

13 × 9 × 2-inch rectangle	40 to 45 minutes
15½ × 10½ × 1-inch jelly roll	30 to 35 minutes
two 8 × 1½-inch rounds	40 to 45 minutes
two 9 × 1½-inch rounds	35 to 40 minutes

Carrot Cake

1½ cups sugar

1 cup vegetable oil

3 eggs

2 cups all-purpose flour

1½ teaspoons ground cinnamon

1 teaspoon baking soda

1 teaspoon vanilla

½ teaspoon salt

¼ teaspoon ground nutmeg

3 cups shredded carrots (about 5 medium)

1 cup coarsely chopped nuts

Heat oven to 350°. Grease and flour desired pan(s). Mix sugar, oil and eggs in large bowl until blended; beat 1 minute. Stir in remaining ingredients except carrots and nuts; beat 1 minute. Stir in carrots and nuts. Pour batter into pan(s).

Bake as directed below or until toothpick inserted in center comes out clean. Cool 10 minutes; remove from pan(s). Cool completely.

13 × 9 × 2-inch rectangle	35 to 40 minutes
two 8 × 1½-inch rounds	40 to 45 minutes
two 9 × 1½-inch rounds	35 to 40 minutes

APPLE CAKE: Substitute 3 cups chopped tart apples (about 3 medium) for the carrots.

Dark Cocoa Cake

2¼ cups all-purpose flour

1⅔ cups sugar

⅔ cup cocoa

¾ cup shortening

1¼ cups water

1¼ teaspoons baking soda

1 teaspoon salt

¼ teaspoon baking powder

1 teaspoon vanilla

2 eggs

Heat oven to 350°. Grease and flour desired pan(s). Beat all ingredients in large bowl on low speed 30 seconds, scraping bowl constantly. Beat on high speed 3 minutes, scraping bowl occasionally. Pour batter into pan(s).

Bake as directed below or until toothpick inserted in center comes out clean. Cool 10 minutes; remove from pan(s). Cool completely.

13 × 9 × 2-inch rectangle	40 to 45 minutes
two 8 × 1½-inch rounds	35 to 40 minutes
two 9 × 1½-inch rounds	30 to 35 minutes
two 8 × 8 × 2-inch squares	35 to 40 minutes
24 medium 2½ × 1¼-inch muffin cups	20 to 25 minutes

Double Chocolate Cake

2¼ cups all-purpose flour

1¾ cups sugar

½ cup shortening

1½ cups buttermilk

1½ teaspoons baking soda

1 teaspoon salt

1 teaspoon vanilla

2 ounces unsweetened chocolate, melted and cooled

2 eggs

1 cup miniature chocolate chips

Heat oven to 350°. Grease and flour desired pan(s). Beat all ingredients except chocolate chips in large bowl on medium speed 30 seconds, scraping bowl constantly. Beat on high speed 2 minutes, scraping bowl occasionally. Fold in chocolate chips. Pour batter into pan(s).

Bake as directed below or until toothpick inserted in center comes out clean. Cool 10 minutes; remove from pan(s). Cool completely.

13 × 9 × 2-inch rectangle	40 to 45 minutes
two 9 × 5 × 3-inch loaves	35 to 40 minutes
two 8 × 1½-inch rounds	40 to 45 minutes
two 9 × 1½-inch rounds	35 to 40 minutes
two 9 × 9 × 2-inch squares	35 to 40 minutes
24 medium 2½ × 4¼-inch muffin cups	20 to 25 minutes

CHOCOLATE-CHERRY CAKE: Fold in ½ cup chopped maraschino cherries, well drained, with the chocolate chips.

Pound Cake

2 cups all-purpose flour

1 cup sugar

3 teaspoons baking powder

1/2 teaspoon salt

1/4 cup (1/2 stick) margarine or butter, softened

1/4 cup shortening

3/4 cup milk

1 teaspoon vanilla

2 eggs

Heat oven to 300°. Grease and flour desired pan(s). Beat all ingredients in large bowl on medium speed 30 seconds, scraping bowl constantly. Beat on high speed 2 minutes, scraping bowl occasionally. Pour batter into pan(s).

Bake as directed below or until toothpick inserted in center comes out clean. Cool 10 minutes; remove from pan(s). Cool completely.

two 9 × 5 × 3-inch loaves	40 to 45 minutes
1½-quart round casserole	65 to 75 minutes

Pumpkin-Gingerbread Cake

3½ cups all-purpose flour

2 cups sugar

1 cup (2 sticks) margarine or butter, softened

1/2 cup light molasses

1/3 cup water

2 teaspoons baking soda

1 teaspoon salt

1 teaspoon ground cinnamon

1 teaspoon ground ginger

1/2 teaspoon baking powder

1/4 teaspoon ground nutmeg

1/4 teaspoon ground cloves

1 can (16 ounces) pumpkin

4 eggs

Heat oven to 350°. Grease and flour desired pan(s). Beat all ingredients in large bowl on low speed 30 seconds, scraping bowl constantly. Beat on medium speed 3 minutes, scraping bowl occasionally. Pour batter into pan(s).

Bake as directed below or until toothpick inserted in center comes out clean. Cool 10 minutes; remove from pan(s). Cool completely.

13 × 9 × 2-inch rectangle	50 to 55 minutes
two 1½-quart round casseroles	65 to 75 minutes

White Cake

2¼ cups all-purpose flour

1⅔ cups sugar

⅔ cup shortening

1¼ cups milk

3½ teaspoons baking powder

1 teaspoon salt

1 teaspoon vanilla

5 egg whites

Heat oven to 350°. Grease and flour desired pan(s). (Line small muffin cups with paper baking cups.) Beat all ingredients except egg whites in large bowl on low speed 30 seconds, scraping bowl constantly. Beat on high speed 2 minutes, scraping bowl occasionally. Beat in egg whites on high speed 2 minutes, scraping bowl occasionally. Pour batter into pan(s).

Bake as directed below or until toothpick inserted in center comes out clean or until cake springs back when touched lightly in center. Cool 10 minutes; remove from pan(s). Cool completely.

13 × 9 × 2-inch rectangle	40 to 45 minutes
15½ × 10½ × 1-inch jelly roll	25 to 30 minutes
two 8 × 1½-inch rounds	35 to 40 minutes
two 9 × 1½-inch rounds	30 to 35 minutes
12-cup ovenproof ring mold	35 to 40 minutes
24 medium 2½ × 1¼-inch muffin cups	20 to 25 minutes
12 small 1¾ × 1-inch muffin cups	10 to 15 minutes
8 × 1½-inch round and	30 to 35 minutes
8 × 8 × 2-inch square	30 to 35 minutes

ALMOND CAKE: Substitute 1 teaspoon almond extract for the vanilla.

CHERRY-NUT CAKE: Fold ½ cup chopped nuts and ⅓ cup chopped maraschino cherries, well drained, into batter.

HAZELNUT CAKE: Add 1 cup ground hazelnuts with ingredients.

MARBLE CAKE: Pour half of batter into another bowl. Mix 2 ounces unsweetened chocolate, melted and cooled, 1 tablespoon sugar, 2 tablespoons warm water and ¼ teaspoon baking soda. Stir into one batter. Spoon light and dark batters alternately into pan(s). Cut through batter several times for marbled effect.

PASTEL MARBLE CAKE: Divide batter into 3 equal parts. Tint one part with 2 or 3 drops red food color and one part with 2 or 3 drops green food color; leave other part plain. Spoon batters alternately into pan(s).

Baking Pan Tips

If the recipe makes 36 cupcakes and you have only one 12-cup muffin pan or if you want to make a 3-layer cake and you have only 2 pans, cover and refrigerate the remaining batter while the first cupcakes or layers are baking.

Yellow Cake

2¼ cups all-purpose flour

1½ cups sugar

3½ teaspoons baking powder

1 teaspoon salt

1¼ cups milk

¼ cup (½ stick) margarine or butter, softened

¼ cup shortening

1 teaspoon vanilla

3 eggs

Heat oven to 350°. Grease and flour desired pan(s). Beat all ingredients in large bowl on low speed 30 seconds, scraping bowl constantly. Beat on high speed 3 minutes, scraping bowl occasionally. Pour batter into pan(s).

Bake as directed below or until toothpick inserted in center comes out clean or until cake springs back when touched lightly in center. Cool 10 minutes; remove from pan(s). Cool completely.

13 × 9 × 2-inch rectangle	40 to 45 minutes
two 8 × 1½-inch rounds	30 to 35 minutes
two 9 × 1½-inch rounds	30 to 35 minutes
two 9 × 1½-inch hearts	25 to 30 minutes
2-quart round casserole	65 to 75 minutes
12 medium 2½ × 1¼-inch muffin cups and	20 to 25 minutes
9 × 9 × 2-inch square	30 to 35 minutes

ORANGE-COCONUT CAKE: Omit vanilla. Add 1 tablespoon grated orange peel and 1 cup flaked coconut with ingredients.

LEMON–POPPY SEED CAKE: Omit vanilla. Add 1 tablespoon grated lemon peel and 2 tablespoons poppy seed with ingredients.

Buttercream Frosting

8 cups powdered sugar

1 cup (2 sticks) margarine or butter, softened

1 cup shortening

⅓ cup milk

2 teaspoons vanilla or almond extract

Beat powdered sugar, margarine and shortening in large bowl on low speed until blended. Beat in milk and vanilla on medium speed until smooth. If necessary, stir in milk, a few drops at a time, until of spreading consistency. *About 6 cups.*

Chocolate Decorator Frosting

1 square (1 ounce) unsweetened chocolate, chopped

1 teaspoon margarine or butter

1 cup powdered sugar

1 to 2 tablespoons boiling water

Heat chocolate and margarine in 1-quart saucepan over low heat until melted; remove from heat. Blend in powdered sugar and 1 tablespoon water. Beat until smooth. Beat in additional water, 1 teaspoon at a time, until of spreading consistency. *About 1 cup.*

Creamy Chocolate Frosting

½ cup (1 stick) margarine or butter, softened

3 ounces unsweetened chocolate, melted and cooled

3 cups powdered sugar

2 teaspoons vanilla

About 3 tablespoons milk

Mix margarine and chocolate in large bowl. Stir in powdered sugar. Beat in vanilla and milk until smooth and of spreading consistency. *About 2¼ cups.*

CREAMY COCOA FROSTING: Substitute ½ cup cocoa for the chocolate.

Creamy Vanilla Frosting

5½ cups powdered sugar

⅔ cup margarine or butter, softened

2 teaspoons vanilla

About 3 tablespoons milk

Mix powdered sugar and margarine in large bowl. Stir in vanilla and milk. Beat until smooth and of spreading consistency. *About 3 cups.*

CREAMY ALMOND FROSTING: Substitute 1½ teaspoons almond extract for the vanilla.

CREAMY CITRUS FROSTING: Omit vanilla. Substitute lemon or orange juice for the milk. Stir in ½ teaspoon grated lemon peel or 2 teaspoons grated orange peel.

PEANUT BUTTER FROSTING: Substitute peanut butter for the margarine. Increase milk to ¼ to ⅓ cup.

Creamy White Frosting

Regular vanilla extract will work in this recipe, but clear vanilla will make for a whiter frosting. It is available at larger supermarkets or specialty baking shops.

6 cups powdered sugar

¾ cup shortening

Milk

¾ teaspoon clear vanilla or almond extract

Mix powdered sugar and shortening in large bowl. Beat in milk and vanilla until smooth. If necessary, stir in milk, a few drops at a time, until of spreading consistency. *About 4 cups.*

Cream Cheese Frosting

1 package (8 ounces) cream cheese, softened

1 tablespoon milk

1 teaspoon vanilla

4 cups powdered sugar

Beat cream cheese, milk and vanilla in large bowl on low speed until smooth. Gradually beat in powdered sugar, 1 cup at a time, until smooth and of spreading consistency. Refrigerate any remaining frosted cake. *About 2½ cups.*

Easy Penuche Frosting

½ cup (1 stick) margarine or butter
1 cup packed brown sugar
¼ cup milk
2 cups powdered sugar

Heat margarine in 1½-quart saucepan over low heat until melted. Stir in brown sugar. Heat to boiling, stirring constantly. Boil and stir over low heat 2 minutes. Stir in milk. Heat to boiling; remove from heat. Cool to lukewarm. Gradually stir in powdered sugar. Place saucepan in bowl of ice and water; beat until of spreading consistency. If frosting becomes too stiff, heat slightly, stirring constantly. *About 2 cups.*

White Decorator Frosting

6¼ cups powdered sugar
¾ cup shortening
½ cup milk
¾ teaspoon clear vanilla or almond extract

Mix powdered sugar and shortening. Beat in milk and vanilla until smooth. If necessary, stir in additional milk, a few drops at a time, until of spreading consistency. *About 4 cups.*

White Mountain Frosting

½ cup sugar
¼ cup light corn syrup
2 tablespoons water
2 egg whites
1 teaspoon vanilla

Mix sugar, corn syrup and water in 1-quart saucepan. Cover and heat to rolling boil over medium heat. Uncover and boil rapidly to 242° on candy thermometer (or until small amount of mixture dropped into very cold water forms a firm ball that holds its shape until pressed).

As mixture boils, beat egg whites in medium bowl just until stiff peaks form. Pour hot syrup very slowly in thin stream into egg whites, beating constantly on medium speed. Add vanilla; beat on high speed until stiff peaks form. *About 3 cups.*

Note: To get an accurate temperature reading on the thermometer, it may be necessary to tilt the saucepan slightly. It takes 4 to 8 minutes for the syrup to reach 242°. Preparing this type of frosting on a humid day may require a longer beating time.

FLUFFY BROWN SUGAR FROSTING: Substitute packed brown sugar for the granulated sugar and decrease vanilla to ½ teaspoon.

FLUFFY COCOA FROSTING: Sift ¼ cup cocoa over frosting and fold in until blended.

FLUFFY CITRUS FROSTING: Substitute 1 teaspoon finely shredded orange or lemon peel for the vanilla.

Chocolate Glaze

1 package (6 ounces) semisweet choco-
late chips
1/4 cup (1/2 stick) margarine or butter
2 tablespoons light corn syrup

Heat all ingredients over low heat, stirring constantly, until chocolate chips are melted and mixture is smooth and of drizzling consistency. Cool slightly. *About 1 cup.*

White Chocolate Glaze

1/2 cup vanilla milk chips
2 tablespoons light corn syrup
1 1/2 teaspoons water

Heat all ingredients over low heat, stirring constantly, until vanilla chips are melted and mixture is smooth and of drizzling consistency. Cool slightly. *About 1/2 cup.*

Petits Fours Glaze

8 cups powdered sugar
1/2 cup water
1/2 cup light corn syrup
2 teaspoons almond extract

Mix all ingredients in top of double boiler until smooth. Heat just until lukewarm; remove from heat. Let glaze remain over hot water to prevent thickening. If necessary, add hot water, a few drops at a time, for desired consistency. *About 4 cups glaze.*

Index